The Making of the
Canadian Media

McGRAW-HILL RYERSON SERIES IN CANADIAN SOCIOLOGY

GENERAL EDITOR — LORNE TEPPERMAN
Department of Sociology
University of Toronto

DEMOGRAPHIC BASES OF CANADIAN SOCIETY
Warren Kalbach and Wayne McVey
(Revision due Spring, 1978)

A STATISTICAL PROFILE OF CANADIAN SOCIETY
Daniel Kubat and David Thornton

IDEOLOGICAL PERSPECTIVES ON CANADA
M. Patricia Marchak

SOCIAL MOBILITY IN CANADA
Lorne Tepperman

THE CANADIAN CLASS STRUCTURE
Dennis Forcese

CANADIAN SOCIETY IN HISTORICAL PERSPECTIVE
S. D. Clark

**THE DISREPUTABLE PLEASURES: CRIME AND
DEVIANCE IN CANADA**
John Hagan

CRIME CONTROL: THE URGE TOWARD AUTHORITY
Lorne Tepperman

UNDERSTANDING DATA
B. H. Erickson and T. A. Nosanchuk

THE MAKING OF THE CANADIAN MEDIA
Paul Rutherford

Forthcoming

SOCIAL CHANGE IN CANADA
Lorna Marsden and Edward Harvey

URBAN ETHNIC COMMUNITIES
Jeffrey G. Reitz

SOCIAL PSYCHOLOGY AS POLITICAL ECONOMY
W. P. Archibald

CANADIAN FAMILIES IN COMPARATIVE PERSPECTIVE
S. Parvez Wakil

The Making of the Canadian Media

Paul Rutherford

Department of History
University of Toronto

McGRAW-HILL RYERSON LIMITED
Toronto   Montreal   New York   St. Louis   San Francisco
Auckland   Bogotá   Düsseldorf   Johannesburg   London
Madrid   Mexico   New Delhi   Panama   Paris   São Paulo
Singapore   Sydney   Tokyo

Hardcover ISBN: 0-07-082653-6   Softcover ISBN: 0-07-082559-9

1 2 3 4 5 6 7 8 9 10   AP   7 6 5 4 3 2 1 0 9 8

Printed and bound in Canada

Canadian Cataloguing in Publication Data

Rutherford, Paul, 1944-
    The making of the Canadian media

(McGraw-Hill Ryerson series in Canadian sociology)

Bibliography: p.
ISBN 0-07-082653-6 bd.   ISBN 0-07-082559-9 pa.

1. Mass media - Canada - History. I. Title.

P92.C3R88   301.16'1'0971   C77-001526-3

The extract from an article by Max Rosenfeld on page 77 is reprinted with the permission of Maclean's Magazine.

CONTENTS

Editor's Introduction

At a time when the efforts of social science so often criticize the way things are, the appearance of a resolutely cheerful analysis cannot fail to catch our attention. Paul Rutherford has written such a book about the "making of the media" in Canada, and it is a pleasure to introduce it to what will surely be a large and enthusiastic audience.

This book has many virtues. At the outset one is provoked by the author's acknowledgement of an "addiction" to the media; this fellow is a fan and he is enjoying himself, almost daring us to say otherwise. His telling of this story, admittedly personal, emphasizes certain topics in the growth of the media (notably the rise of newspapers) and underplays others. This is an elegantly written and enjoyable book, a book rich in new information, new insight and synthesis. Further these qualities are bonuses, since the book is the most complete ever on the history of the mass media in Canada. It must be read by anyone with a serious interest in the subject.

Professor Rutherford concludes that, from the beginning, the mass media helped to cultivate an "open society" in Canada. He shows how the media made us liberal, even if capitalistic; cosmopolitan, even if dominated by foreign ideas; and relatively united in our thoughts and action, even if united only as an impersonal mass audience. To state the case differently, being Canadian means living within limitations imposed by our economy and by historical relations of dependency. The mass media do not remove those limitations, and probably they cannot; but they make Canada as "open" a society as can be expected.

To this end, the author shows how journalism changed from rather uncritical partisanship to something like a craft, and finally into a profession, with a measure of independence and social responsibility. Starting out as unstable, bickering protégés of the powerful, the media owners created an industry of national and international scope, having undoubted influence on government policy. Canadian culture and the national identity develop alongside the media in this story. "Public opinion" emerges through the reciprocal influences of the mass media upon the people, and the people upon the media. The history of the mass media is here a focus for the history of Canadian nation-building.

This book is an excellent example of how historical materials and argument can be used to analyse social institutions, making it particularly valuable to sociologists and historians. To others seeking to understand the growth of an institution (that now leaves no one's life untouched) I recommend this book on the mass media as an inventive and refreshing piece of reading.

Lorne Tepperman

Introduction

This book explores the history of the communications media in Canada. It soothes a very personal itch. While not a member of McLuhan's TV generation, I have long been a media addict, one of those happy consumers of everything from pulp fiction and rock music to CBC newscasts and the Sunday New York *Times*. Some years back, I decided to delve into the origins of my addiction, or to put that query into more scholarly terms, to investigate the historical significance of communications in Canada. A quick survey of the existing literature soon demonstrated that no one had seriously grappled with the question. True, a decade ago, W. H. Kesterton pioneered in the story of communications with his *A History of Journalism in Canada*. But that work, however valuable, concentrates more on the craft of journalism and the detail of press history. So my book is intended to fill a gap in our understanding of the Canadian experience: to trace the evolution of the media and the impact of communications.

I must make clear two qualifications about the study. First, the book does not attempt to apply to the history of the media any theory or model concocted by a great thinker. Historians are notorious for their suspicion of grand theories — it is part of their charm (and no doubt a source of contempt) in an academic world afflicted by hardening of the mind. Now, I cannot deny that my work has been conditioned by the findings of communications theorists. Some readers may well discover echoes of the philosophy of Harold Innis and Marshall McLuhan, in particular their emphasis upon the cultural importance of communications systems. More obviously, I have drawn ideas from the excellent sociological literature on the mass media, especially with regard to the limits and the extent of media power. (In passing, I might note that the most enlightening of the treatises I found was Denis McQuail's brief survey, *Towards a Sociology of Mass Communications*.) Even so, whatever theory underlies this survey is eclectic and haphazard, derived as much from the facts of history as the musings of social scientists.

Secondly, the book does not pretend to be the final word. Most of the arguments rest upon a reading of the enormous wealth of reminiscences, accounts, criticisms, reports, and monographs pertinent to the development of the media. Only to fill holes in the findings of these sources have I engaged in primary research. Besides, I have fixed my attention upon certain media. Commonsense alone suggests the most ubiquitous media have always been the press, joined recently by radio and television. So my work concentrates first upon daily newspapers and eventually upon this big three, stopping briefly where necessary to delve into the story of magazines, books, movies, and the like. What all this means is that the observations which festoon the pages of the survey are often tentative and speculative. A more scholarly, comprehensive treatment of the communications media must await a full-scale investigation of all the sources available, a project for the years ahead. This book represents my interpretation of what has already been discovered.

Every self-respecting book needs a thesis. To my mind, the media do constitute a special institution, better yet a fourth estate which has played an important if changing role in Canadian life. That presumption has led me to organize the story of communications in three essays that comprehend the outstanding stages in the growth of media influence. Each essay deals perforce with the nitty-gritty of media history in order to portray the actual character of the institution. In addition, each relates the media to the salient features of the Canadian experience to show the impact of communications. The opening essay, "The Rise of the Newspaper," gallops through the first century or so, from the British Conquest to Confederation, when Canada gained both a mature press and an open society. The second essay, "The Golden Age of the Press," covering the next sixty years up to the Depression, looks at the supremacy of the big city daily and the impact of mass communications upon the ways of early industrial Canada. The last essay, "The Triumph of the Multimedia", taking the story up to the present day, probes the nature of the aforementioned big three and the affluent society they have conditioned. The "Conclusion" merely supplies assorted comments on the study of communications, including its pitfalls. "A Media Bibliography" lists those published sources which I found most useful or stimulating. The bibliography should guide the reader in his search for material on specific aspects of media history.

This book is opinionated history. Sometimes the survey takes on the aspect of a history of Canada written solely from the perspective of communications. That is necessary to highlight the significance of the media. I do not mean to suggest, however, that the media have been any more central to the course of Canadian development than the business community, political parties, the churches, the family or, for that matter, the men's clubs. Furthermore, the discussion of the Canadian media reflects my own libertarian outlook. The reader will likely find the book a sympathetic, even conservative appraisal of the media, especially the present multimedia. Which brings me back to my opening lines: I am an addict, not a critic, of mass communications. I think the media have been and remain, to replay an old cliché, on the side of the angels. This book stands as a personal justification of my addiction; perhaps it will lead other people to admit the benefits of the vast cornucopia of delights our media dispense.

One last comment. No enterprise of this sort is possible without the encouragement and assistance of kind souls. I thank the Canada Council and the University of Toronto for the funds that allowed me a sabbatical leave to study the literature on the Canadian media. I am grateful to Lorne Tepperman, who persuaded me to write the book; Ruth McLean, who was a friend as well as a research assistant; the staff of the Newspaper Room at the National Library in Ottawa, who have made profitable my many research forays; Ramsay Cook and Thelma McCormack, whose criticisms aided the revision of the manuscript. My work has depended most on Gail Rutherford; she not only laboured to keep the household and kids in order so that I could write, but acted as a sympathetic audience for various ideas in the process of developing my arguments. This book is dedicated, with all my love, to Gail.

I

Ironically, an earlier generation of tory officials had encouraged the foundation of the press. The printing press came to Canada in the 1750s and 1760s with the British conqueror. Already in Europe, the printing press had a history of some three hundred years, going back to the invention of movable types by Johann Gutenberg in the mid-fifteenth century. From Germany, printing soon spread throughout western and southern Europe, including France. But the state and church in France remained suspicious of the power of printing, all too aware this power could be turned against established authority. French officials therefore opposed the introduction into New France of a printing press which, distances being so great, they could never properly regulate. Whatever printing might be necessary to satisfy colonial needs could be done at home. Consequently, even though there was sporadic pressure for a printing press within the colony, the officials and churchmen of New France were deprived of the advantages and spared the worries the printing press brought their counterparts in the American colonies.

British rulers were more lenient. In Britain, printing early established itself as a vital adjunct of religion, commerce, literature, and even politics. True, the state had some troubles with printers, even executing a couple for sedition. But, by and large, the authorities felt able to discipline printing and publishing. Likewise, in the New World, British officials accepted the virtues of printing, though on occasion taking harsh action to curb the excesses of recalcitrant publishers. This attitude allowed the emergence of a rich and varied literary tradition which made the Thirteen Colonies a home of intellectual ferment, ultimately disastrous to British rule. Still, when the Empire consumed Canada, nothing seemed more natural than the introduction of the printing press to aid in the task of development and civilization. Thus in 1791, John Graves Simcoe, newly appointed Lieutenant-Governor of the wilderness colony of Upper Canada, claimed "a printer is indispensibly necessary."[2] The presence of a printer would, so it seemed, contribute mightily to the conversion of Upper Canada into a tory bastion of British power.

Whatever the official attitude, however, the actual expansion of printing depended upon the efforts of private entrepreneurs. No wonder, then, that native print media grew slowly. Market conditions were hardly ideal. Outside of the leading towns, there was little call for printed matter. For many years, much of the population, especially in Québec, was not even literate. A good portion of the demand for books and magazines could be met by foreign imports. So, as late as 1800, there were just nine active printing establishments across the length and breadth of British America. In succeeding decades, of course, the increased tempo of colonial development enhanced the business opportunities for newcomers to the printing and publishing trades. Indeed, after the War of 1812, the spread of the printing press was spectacular. The bumptious metropoli that endeavoured to reign over their colonies boasted four, five, and sometimes more printers and publishers. In Toronto in 1840, for example, there were four bookseller-publishers: the Lesslie brothers, Henry Rowsell, Hugh Scobie, and Egerton Ryerson — as well as other journalists who might publish the occasional piece. By this time, their colleagues had arrived in the numerous lesser towns which dotted the colonial countryside. A native literary culture had taken shape throughout Canada.

This culture had remained peculiarly unbalanced, at least by comparison with the European and American varieties. Canadian publishers had not nurtured an indigenous literature of entertainment. There was little in the way of a Canadian "belles-lettres." True, especially after 1820, some Canadians did author and publish novels and notably poetry, though with a very few exceptions these works were derivative, their merit slight, and their appeal minute. Similarly, while small coteries of optimists launched literary magazines, modelled upon foreign types, time and again they failed to sustain these endeavours in the face of the indifference, even disdain, of the educated, genteel public. One hopeful, Michel Bibaud, actually started five different reviews between 1817 and 1842, none very successful. More important than the lack of a Canadian "belles-lettres" was the lack of a Canadian "trash" — a cheap, popular product for the ordinary reader. Elsewhere, publishers supplied homegrown ballads, legends, satires, poetry, novels, indeed anything that might capture the public's attention. Not so, or not often in Canada. The void was filled by foreign works, whether reprinted by Canadian publishers or imported from outside. By mid-century, the market for books and magazines in Upper Canada was largely the preserve of American publishers of cheap American works and British reprints. The growth of a magazine press and a national literature had been hamstrung, and by the preferences of readers whatever their race or station. Thus was established what has become a great Canadian tradition: a parasitical dependence upon the dreams, the romances, the adventures, the tragedies, the plays, the epics, all the stuff of fancy and fantasy, manufactured by outsiders. Such, of course, was the lot of a colony.

By contrast, the native publishing industry soon produced a rich variety of works detailing the routine of the real world, works which, however derivative, were stamped as uniquely "Canadian." The thrust of most Canadian imprints was decidedly utilitarian. Much the publisher supplied could never expect a wide market, though subsidies made its printing profitable: laws and regulations, government proclamations, journals of the assembly, commercial notices, the constitutions and proceedings of associations, and the like. Still, from the beginning, he produced material with a popular appeal. The earliest, and

for almost a century the most important staple of the publisher's offerings was the almanac, a yearly compendium of facts practical and
weird. Slower to appear in large numbers, yet of increasing importance
as profitable ventures, were primers and grammars for children;
travel-books and tourist guides; practical manuals of commercial, agricultural, or medical lore; business directories and gazetteers; and
eventually advanced school texts, histories, and biographies. Francophone publishers early specialized in devotional literature —
catechisms, prayer books, lives of saints, little homilies — which
popularized the teachings of religion. Anglophone publishers, following in the footsteps of their British and American mentors, printed
accounts of murders and trials complete with the last thoughts of the
criminal or his relatives, a type of true confession which catered to the
ever-present taste for sensationalism amongst the public, the genteel as
well as the rabble. Numbered among the remnant in publishers' lists
were such items as cookbooks (the first such publication, in 1831,
sported the marvellous title "The Cook Not Mad"), collections of
folklore, amateur treatises on botany or geology, and assorted sports
trivia.

What was especially remarkable, though, was the rise and fall of the
pamphlet as a medium of controversy in public affairs. The first species
of such polemic was really the sermon, signal proof of the privileged
status the clergy enjoyed in early Canada. The clergy took upon themselves the task of determining the outlook of the public and officialdom. The most important sermons came from the bishops of the leading, almost established churches — Anglican, Presbyterian, Congrega-
tional, and Roman Catholic. These sermons were stridently tory.
Churchmen emphasized the utility of religion, sang the blessings of a
structured society, pleaded for social harmony, and urged the virtues of
morality. Just as fervently, they lavished praise upon Britain, its
superiority assumed, condemned the foreign demons of revolution and
democracy, and slandered the enemies of civilization, primarily
Napoleonic France and Republican America. With the collapse of the
tory order after the Rebellions, the political bishop lost a good deal of
his significance, indeed his raison d'être. Sermons were still published,
but on the whole they were devoted to lesser questions of doctrinal
dispute or pious declarations on Christian morality. Only in Québec
did the tory tradition of episcopal sermonizing continue, revitalized by
the ultramontane bishops in their mandements.

Long before the eclipse of the tory sermons, their role had been challenged, initially by election ephemera — declarations, letters, advertisements, songs, satires, and denunciations. Appearing in the 1790s
but more common after the turn of the century, such matter always
enjoyed a vogue when there was a hotly disputed election in the offing.
Unlike the sermons, election ephemera were more personal, more immediate, and more diverse. Any and all zealots could employ the

medium to purvey their particular crotchets or bile. In 1810 in Québec, for instance, there were published two anonymous "chansons," both sung to popular tunes: the first, a Jacobinical cry against the vile establishment and its myrmidons in parliament; the second, a gloating tory dirge on the disarray of the radical forces. This matter informed, cajoled, angered, and diverted the populace. Still, election ephemera were a limited medium, local and temporary in impact. Though they lasted throughout the nineteenth century, their significance was never great in public debate, whatever their importance in individual contests.

Both the tory sermon and election ephemera were superseded by the political pamphlet itself. Pamphlets had appeared at a very early stage in the history of publishing. But their heyday occurred during the turbulent years between the War of 1812 and the Rebellions of 1837. Pamphlets were easy to produce and distribute, therefore excellent as a means of swaying the opinions of small publics. No wonder all manner of partisans, from the high tory to the republican democrat, on all manner of topics, from the character of government to the state of trade, used pamphlets to engage in polemic. Yet after the Rebellions, pamphlets also declined in significance, though not in numbers. Political excitements, such as those surrounding the annexation crisis of 1849-50 or the Confederation debates of the mid-1860s, were guaranteed to inspire a flood of pamphlets. And other kinds of publicists, like railway promoters or temperance advocates, employed the pamphlet to get across their messages. But, by mid-century, pamphlet literature was fast becoming the medium of the eccentric. All that was required was a sense of mission, an ability to write, and a little money. Such a situation ensured the survival of pamphlet literature, but rendered that literature largely impotent as a medium of serious controversy. For the target of the pamphlet was the converted, those already convinced of the import or truth of the cause purveyed. Public debate was the province of the newspaper.

II

Nothing, not the pamphlet, the book, or the magazine could compare in significance with the newspaper. Contemporaries recognized this. Susannah Moodie, an early chronicler of Canadian customs, wryly noted "the Canadian cannot get on without his newspaper any more than an American could without his tobacco."[3] Perhaps so, but the newspaper had not gained its pre-eminence without a struggle. The first newspapers, invariably entitled "gazettes," were in fact pretty timid affairs, largely because of their proprietors. These men were the first printers on the scene, generally American trained, who came in search of a secure and profitable business career — or were driven northwards by the victory of the American rebels. Christopher Sower, made King's Printer for New Brunswick in 1785, had been a British spy during the Revolution. Publishing a gazette was expected, and necessary to win official and public patronage, even if the newspaper lost money. But these ventures did not make their proprietors journalists, at least not in the normal sense. They produced weekly four page collections of government proclamations, foreign news, a few ads, and occasional trivia. Indeed, these gazettes constituted an official press, instinctively tory though more turgid than opinionated. Their role was to inform the small, literate elite of the affairs of the world. After the turn of the century, the gazettes were shunted aside by new competition, some disappearing while others were transformed into political papers.

The so-called free press actually originated with the unofficial newspaper, which by definition lacked a direct link to the ruling oligarchy. The first such journal, Anthony Henry's short-lived Halifax Chronicle (1769-1770), was launched because its proprietor, erstwhile King's Printer and manager of the local gazette, had lost official favour. That did not mean the unofficial newspaper was in any way the people's champion. Far from it. Invariably, the hopeful proprietor searched for a "connection," a constituency whose needs he might serve and whose patronage he would receive. Not surprisingly, his connection was normally with some branch of the local establishment. Before long, newspapers had been founded for the leading Loyalists of Halifax and St. John, the radical-minded literati of Montréal, the "English" party and the "French" party of Québec City — and, strange as it might seem, the English, American, and Scottish merchants of Montréal. Some of these papers did indulge in polemic. Fleury Mesplet's Gazette littéraire (1778-1779) took upon itself the task of bringing the wisdom of Voltaire to bear upon the sadly deficient institutions of Québec, a mission which soon brought down the wrath of the authorities upon the heads of its owner and editor. John Ryan's St. John Gazette (1785) briefly espoused the cause of Loyalist assemblymen against the British-born officials. Pierre Bédard's Le Canadien (1806) engaged in ferocious, long-winded controversies with anglophone racists and tories. Such partisan fervour, of course, was rare. The unofficial newspaper more often displayed a studied neutrality in matters of local contention.

The next generation of journalists, following the War of 1812, discovered the joys of partisan warfare. New journals were started to publicize some definite perspective upon public affairs. Among the first were two Halifax newspapers, Anthony Holland's Acadian Recorder (1813) for the emerging reform element which quickly inspired a pro-government rival, Edmund Ward's Free Press (1816). Established journals were drawn into the fray. The rare proprietor who tried to remain neutral soon fell by the wayside. Thus in Kingston, Stephen Miles, owner of the unofficial Gazette (1810-1818), was forced out of business because he failed to take a firm stand in opposition to Robert Gourlay's radical agitation. This steady politicization of the press brought to each city, and eventually many small towns as well, the boon of at least two newspapers, one boldly Reform and the other equally Tory. During the 1840s and 1850s, the surviving newspapers, plus another crew of newcomers, were transformed into party organs, sometimes marshalled into provincial networks. Long before this, however, the press had reached the stage of critical mass. First the politicization, but even more the proliferation of newspapers had given substance to that already hackneyed phrase, "the power of the press." By the 1830s, the very numbers of journals and journalists had made the press a force in the politics of the land.

Linked to the proliferation of newspapers was a parallel phenomenon, the diversification of the press. The most prominent newspapers were the various party organs in the provincial centres. Most enjoyed some circulation in the countryside, hence becoming early agents of metropolitanism. But they soon acquired rivals. A vigorous country press first appeared in Ontario in the late 1820s and early 1830s, more slowly in the rest of Canada (especially French Québec), to cater to local interests and mayhap counter urban propaganda. Within the cities emerged a variety of commercial newssheets, serving more the economic than the political needs of the business community. As early as the mid-1830s, some newcomers to journalism attempted to create a cheap "popular" press, already very successful in England and the United States, which would reach a family audience — especially, so it would seem, the bourgeois housewife.[4] They were later joined by dour sectarian warriors, first sponsored by Irish Catholic and soon French Catholic militants, designed to fight the good battle for God and Race.[5] The latter type, the ultramontane newspaper was supposed to emulate Louis Veuillot's L'Univers, a furious combatant devoted to refuting the errors manufactured by the liberal and radical press of France. Another French import was the satirical journal of combat brought to Québec by Napoléon Aubin in 1837. His initial success with Le Fantasque(1837-1849) inspired a host of imitators, none so witty, and in later decades this genre sadly deteriorated. By the 1840s and 1850s, there flourished as well a "class" press catering to a wide range of special interests, notably agriculture and business, the major sects and churches, law, medicine, and education, temperance and moral reform, even fraternal associations. So by mid-century, the Canadian reader could select from a veritable supermarket of newspaper delights.

What completed this consumer's paradise was the arrival of the daily newspaper. The daily, common elsewhere at the turn of the century, came late to Canada. Not until the 1840s was the climate ripe for a daily press. By then, the new cities ensured a market for the wares of the daily journalist, and the busy retail trade of these cities enhanced his all-important advertising revenues. Stagecoaches in the 1830s, the steamships in the 1840s, and railways in the 1850s speeded the transmission of news and the distribution of newspapers. Equally important, the spread of telegraph lines after the mid-1840s linked newspaper offices to the sources of news, thereby furnishing the journalist daily with a fresh commodity. Indeed, that great feat of Victorian engineering, the laying of the Atlantic cable in 1866, brought Canadian newspapers into close contact with the exciting events transpiring in the European arena.

In addition, the mechanics of journalism were revolutionized by a series of technological innovations. Printing had changed little during the first three hundred years. The printing press John Bushell first employed in Halifax in 1752 differed only slightly from Gutenberg's invention. This cumbersome, hand-operated, wooden machine required the labours of two men to produce some 200 to 250 impressions per hour. After 1800, inventors in England and America perfected the iron, hand-operated press and the power-driven cylinder press, both much more efficient. Even so, the mechanization of Canadian printing only occurred during the late 1840s and early 1850s. George Brown, the first giant of the daily press, was himself a Canadian agent for Richard Hoe and Company, a major American manufacturer of the new machines. By Confederation, Brown's *Globe* and the rival *Leader*, both of Toronto, were printed by multiple cylinder, power-driven presses capable of throwing off thousands of sheets an hour.

About this time, the other bottleneck, papermaking, was overcome. That too was a slow, tedious business of hand manufacture from the pulp of linen rags. The result: good but expensive paper, rarely in sufficient quantities. Early proprietors were always in search of foreign supplies of cheap, plentiful paper. After 1800, the establishment of native paper mills, fostered by journalists like Anthony Holland, William Lyon Mackenzie, and George Brown, eased the pressure but hardly provided a final solution in colonies where used linen rags were not a common household item. Yet by the 1850s, Europeans had pretty well solved the problems of mechanizing papermaking and of manufacturing paper from wood pulp. At long last, during the late 1860s and early 1870s, Canada's paper industry, following the lead of the Riordon brothers of St. Catherines, fully mechanized its mills and converted to wood-pulp production. The consequence was a flood of inferior but cheap newsprint, more than sufficient to meet the needs of the dailies. The technological basis necessary for a mass press was in place in Canada by 1870.

Even so, the progress of the daily was more cautious than triumphant. Much depended upon the locality — its size, wealth, literacy, and interests. As late as the 1830s, almost all newspapers, whether in towns or cities, were weeklies. The pioneer dailies were two newcomers to already cluttered newspaper markets, the Montreal *Daily Advertiser* (1833) and the Toronto *Royal Standard* (1836), both dismal failures. More successful were the cheap "popular" tri-weeklies, like the Montreal *Transcript* (1836-1865) and the St. John *News* (1839-1884).

Their achievement inspired their more staid rivals to convert to tri-weekly issuance during the next decade. But the first prosperous dailies were two old Montréal newspapers, the *Gazette* and the *Herald*, which after some careful experimentation in the summer months took the plunge in the early 1840s. Their great advantage was a close connection with the anglophone merchants of the city who found up-to-date commercial information very useful.

Thereafter, the centre of activity shifted to Upper Canada. During the 1850s and 1860s, this province experienced an almost continuous boom fueled by immigration, railway construction, and industrialization. The good times engendered a dynamic confidence in all lines of business, not the least being journalism. First in Kingston, then in Toronto, and soon in Hamilton, London, and Ottawa, converted or new dailies swept aside all competition. By the end of the boom, dailies had actually been established in St. Catharines, Guelph, Brantford, and Belleville.

Elsewhere in British America, journalists proved much more hesitant. No other province experienced so extensive a boom. Leading anglophone newspapers in Montréal and Québec City did convert during the 1850s and early 1860s. Maritime bi-weeklies and tri-weeklies, of which there was an incredible profusion, only began the conversion during the mid-1860s. Especially reluctant were the francophone journalists, perhaps because their advertising patrons were less generous. Nonetheless, by the mid-1870s, they too had followed suit. The urban daily now reigned supreme. Rowell's *American Newspaper Directory* of 1873 listed forty-eight daily newspapers across Canada, over half located in Ontario.

Publishing an urban newspaper was by then a big business, and a ruthless one at times. Initially, the task of running a newspaper was not especially onerous. There was, after all, little competition. The first gazettes and their unofficial rivals managed to co-exist amicably. But this happy condition, at least for the proprietors, did not last much beyond 1800. The flowering of the press rendered the newspaper business decidedly insecure. Throughout, it remained ridiculously easy to establish a new paper: in 1869, for instance, Hugh Graham and G. T. Lanigan needed only a few hundred dollars, old equipment, and a bit of goodwill to launch the daily *Star* in Montréal. The problem was to survive. Most newspapers had only a brief life span. Take the example of London: of twenty-odd journals founded between 1830 and 1867, only four existed after Confederation. London was hardly unique. Every city was a newspaper graveyard. The first cause of newspaper troubles was the very clutter of competitors in each market. As late as 1864, Halifax boasted eight different newspapers, all vying to reach much the same public. Only in Toronto, where a fierce struggle during the 1850s left George Brown's *Globe* and James Beaty's *Leader* victorious, was the newspaper scene rationalized, though just for a decade.

The second cause was the enormous increase in the costs of publishing, especially for a successful newspaper. Labour: the weekly pay list of the Montreal *Witness* shot up from $80 in 1860 to $925 by 1877. Equipment: whereas in 1850 John Simpson of the New Brunswick *Royal Gazette* was able to purchase a new steam-driven press for the princely sum of £600, two decades later the eight-cylinder Hoe power press the *Witness* needed cost $30,000. And paper: in 1869, the Riordon company forwarded to the *Globe* office paper valued at $50,000 and in 1870 that figure rose to $60,000. Little wonder that Maurice Laframboise, a well-off Liberal, could lose some $30,000 between 1872 and 1874 in his effort to maintain *Le National* in the crowded (and Conservative) Montréal market.

The logic of his situation forced many a journalist to scramble to find money. All, of course, eagerly sought job-printing contracts from business and government. Most endeavoured to build up their circulation lists, and thereby to generate more revenue from street sales, subscriptions, and advertising. So proprietors offered new subscribers a cut rate or a gift. During the 1860s, John Livingston, proprietor of the new St. John *Telegraph*, offered to people who organized a club of twenty subscribers a free year's copy of *Godey's Lady's Book*, *Harper's Monthly Magazine*, or their equivalent. More and more newcomers entered the evening field to capture a wider audience, especially of women and artisans. In 1861, James Beaty started a one-cent evening edition of his Toronto *Leader* for the same purpose. Newspapers constantly advertised (even occasionally in the columns of a rival) their own virtues. Sometimes this "puffery" was justified. George Brown's *Globe* and later John Livingston's *Telegraph* won kudos and subscribers because they delivered on the promise to specialize in news. Dailies hired groups of newsboys and contracted with local stores to better serve the urban populace. The success of the Montreal *Witness* in the early 1860s was a result of its widespread sale, at the price of one cent, by newsboys. Nor did proprietors neglect readers outside the city. Usually a daily newspaper offered a weekly or a tri-weekly edition, sometimes both, to readers in nearby towns and the countryside. From the beginning of his career in 1844, George Brown strove mightily to reach a provincial audience. For a time, he financed what was called the *Western Globe* in London. Throughout, he used the *Weekly Globe*, with extra matter suitable for country tastes, to appeal to readers in rural Ontario. In 1864, he added the *Canada Farmer*, "a fortnightly journal of agricultural, horticultural and rural affairs."[6] In 1876, he signed with the railways to run early morning editions of the daily *Globe* to Hamilton and London. Similar was the approach of John Dougall, a Montréal proprietor who fathered a little family of newspapers: by 1870, he issued, aside from the daily *Witness*, a tri-weekly edition, a weekly for the Eastern Townships and eastern Ontario, the *Northern Messenger* (a highly successful, semi-monthly, temperance magazine), and the *New Dominion Monthly* (a family magazine).

Such enterprise, however, was rare. The typical proprietor was not an especially imaginative or aggressive entrepreneur. He seemed satisfied with a modicum of success. That fact was reflected in circulation figures (and, given the ethics of the day, even these figures are inflated). In 1873, the average number of copies a Canadian daily sold of all its editions (daily, tri-weekly, and / or weekly) was roughly 5,700. At one extreme were the Montreal *Witness* and the Toronto *Globe*, with combined circulations respectively of 23,000 and 45,000. At the other extreme were papers like the Quebec *Mercury* (1000), the Halifax *Acadian Recorder* (1600), or *Le Journal de Québec* (2200), which by no means exhausts the list. The result was not happy. There were too many newspapers with too few readers. "It may be questioned if this multiplication of journals has not been carried too far, and whether some process of 'natural selection' would not improve those which might be left," admitted an anonymous contemporary. "Fewer and stronger journals, using the telegraph wires more freely, and employing a higher class of talent on their columns, would better meet the requirements of the reading public."[7] Only the newspaper with a healthy circulation list could really be counted sound.

What, then, was the attraction of journalism? Why, the profession seemed such an easy route to comfort and status, if not fame and power. The prospective journalist, after all, needed few special skills, other than the ability to read and write. True, it helped to be a printer. The connection between the so-called profession of journalism and the actual trade of printing lingered to the end of the century, but before long that connection was obviously on the wane in the field of urban journalism. Little wonder the profession attracted a rum lot of rogues, adventurers, dilettantes, crusaders, politicos, and the like. Étienne Parent, editor of *Le Canadien* in its second era of glory during the 1820s and 1830s, was an ex-seminarian drawn to journalism at age twenty by his passionate liberal and nationalist convictions. W. L. Mackenzie was a bored storekeeper who yearned for significance. Adam Thom, the notorious francophobe who edited the Montreal *Herald* in the 1830s, had arrived from Scotland a penniless lawyer. Poverty drove him to journalism to earn his bread, and perchance to make his mark in a new land. By contrast, John Dougall, another Scot but also a successful merchant, thought himself called to journalism by God. Dougall's conversion to evangelical Protestantism inspired him to start the *Witness* to spread the gospel of a purified Christianity to the benighted peoples of Catholic Québec. After 1840, such types were joined by aspiring politicians — Francis Hincks, Joseph Cauchon, Hector Langevin, and William Macdougall, all of whom eventually left the profession for the joys of parliament and government.

By the 1850s and 1860s, though, the profession had taken shape, a rough shape. At the top were the great proprietors of the age, political powers all, like George Brown, Edward Whelan (Charlottetown *Examiner*), or the Annands (Halifax *Chronicle*). Just below were the successful businessmen like James Beaty or George Fenety (St. John *News*) who had attained some wealth and significance. Less fortunate was an underclass of salaried though prominent editors such as George Sheppard, L.-A. Dessaulles, or P. S. Hamilton who never owned their own newspapers. At the bottom was a gaggle of marginal publishers and hack writers whom fate had treated unkindly. Especially poignant was the story of one Samuel Thompson. A Britisher who entered Toronto's printing trades in 1838, he spent the next two decades slowly working his way up in the ranks of the city's press. By the mid-1850s, he was part owner of the *British Colonist*, a major daily newspaper modelled (so Thompson later claimed) upon Britain's "Thunderer," the London *Times*. The grand endeavour proved too expensive. The depression of 1857 almost impoverished him. Desperate, he turned to the government for aid, becoming what amounted to a ministerial publisher. Nothing went right. His last try, the Quebec *Advertiser*, failed in 1860 because of the antagonism of francophone competitors and ministers. Finally, bankrupt, he sold out his interest in the *Advertiser* and surrendered the *Colonist* to James Beaty. Thus, a disconsolate Thompson, a victim of circumstances, passed out of Canadian journalism.

What the profession lacked was a spirit of fraternity. Journalists were not only business competitors but rival partisans. So the public often witnessed editors attacking each other without restraint in their editorial columns. One such round of abuse in 1849 between Ludger Duvernay's *La Minerve* and L.-A. Dessaulles of *L'Avenir* ended up in the courts. Duvernay's journal accused Dessaulles, among other things, of being an atheist. Dessaulles sued for £12,000. The trial, something of a cause célèbre, resulted in a judgement against Duvernay of £100 (a journalist's reputation was never a highly valued item). George Brown, because he was both a party leader and a noted journalist, was the target of almost constant abuse. He was variously described as a Protestant bigot and a French hater (both true, by the way), a democrat and a revolutionary (neither accurate), and a paid American agent. Patrick Boyle of the *Irish Canadian*, much upset by Protestant strength, referred to Brown as "the Cromwell of the House of Assembly,"[8] the leader of the massed forces of Scotch bigotry in Ontario. Occasionally, the name-calling degenerated into actual violence. J. B. E. Dorion, the fiery editor of *Le Défricheur*, known as "l'enfant terrible," charged in the Assembly he had had his face slapped by the editor of Ottawa's *Le Canada*, irate because of some article Dorion had published. Concern over this persistent animosity led to the founding of the Canadian Press

Association in Kingston in 1859. But the CPA was itself hobbled by partisan and business dissensions. Journalists found their friends within their particular political camps.

III

The newspapers these journalists fashioned did have a special character. That Susannah Moodie recognized when she called the Canadian newspaper "a strange mélange of politics, religion, abuse, and general information."[9] Now, in retrospect, the first century or so of press history might seem a glorious era of personal journalism. Later generations of journalists would look back wistfully to this time when editors appeared to enjoy so much freedom. For the typical editor, working with only a few assistants, could easily stamp his image upon the whole newspaper. Its contents were bound to reflect his idiosyncracies. The result was an astonishing variety of offerings. This aside, however, the slight resources the colonial editor had at his disposal made him dependent upon other journalists and publishers. Editors practiced an extraordinary kind of scissors and paste journalism, borrowing or plagiarizing large chunks of each other's prose. Between September 1832 and July 1833, for example, the St. Thomas *Liberal* reprinted articles from at least ninety-two different sources. Magazines or encyclopedias were always useful for a serious piece or two. But many sources were other newspapers; in the case of the *Liberal*, mostly other Reform champions. The practice rested upon the so-called "exchange system," whereby newspapers freely traded issues to ensure a generous supply of information from around the province. Often, the editors also took foreign newspapers, usually American, to provide copy about the outside world. The exchange system was an essential means of transmitting information prior to the arrival of news agencies, and it retained its importance even after the telegraph companies entered the news business in the late 1840s. For not only were other newspapers used to provide detail on topics of interest, but also to supply assorted features and perhaps even an editorial. So an incestuous relationship had grown up among clusters of newspapers, usually defined by province and politics, which checked the eccentric leanings of each journalist.

The colonial newspaper, by comparison with the appearance of the mass newspaper of a later age, was small and dull. Almost always, whether a weekly or a daily, the newspaper was four pages long. Some dailies, like the Toronto *Globe*, became huge "blanket sheets" with pages 30" by 50" of nine columns of closely packed type. But while most newspapers did increase in size after 1830, they averaged around five to seven columns of print per page. The vast majority of the contents were locked into a virtual straitjacket: the print was arrayed in rigid columns, an army of words ready to assault the reader's eye. This formidable appearance was lessened, slightly, by different sizes of type, titles and the occasional headline, and some woodcut illustrations. Usually, the main page was page two, filled with editorials, information, and correspondence. The front page contained a lot of ads, often some news and entertainment, plus assorted overflow material from the inside pages. Pages three and four could be composed of advertisements alone, though normally they carried in addition information and entertainment, perhaps the occasional feature. The actual proportion of these offerings varied with the seasons — ads, for instance, swamped the pages of many urban dailies during the summer months. The news of some gripping event, anything from a war to an election, could dominate all pages. A consistent format never struck the colonial editor as a great virtue.

Advertising consumed between one-third and two-thirds of a newspaper's space. At an early date, the publicity of the newspaper had become a catalyst for all manner of commerce. Most of the advertisements touted the merits of professionals and businessmen, hotels and restaurants, real estate and auctions, eventually steamship and railway lines, as well as a wide assortment of local stores. A range of personal notices and government announcements was likewise usual, though missing at least until the mid-century were many notices of job-openings (especially for the workingman). Fairly common at an early date, however, were ads for tobaccoes, liquors, and patent medicines. But such ads, while lucrative to the proprietor, were held in contempt by the more Victorian of editors because these ads pushed goods that were immoral or dangerous. John Dougall refused to print any ads of a questionable character, including those for theatres, amusements, or distasteful books. From the mid-1850s onwards, urban newspapers slowly eliminated the jumble of advertisements by collecting these under specific headings for the convenience of readers. The Toronto *Globe* of 15 January, 1855 carried sections entitled "Business Directory," "Buffalo Directory," "Montreal Directory," "Hotels," "Real Estate," and "New York Advertisements." It was impressive evidence of the prosperity and variety of Toronto's local economy.

Most ads were bland, informative squibs. They told the reader what was available; they did not attempt to cajole him to use the product or service. John Dougall, indeed, distrusted ads that were too flamboyant, which he felt made for "a very ugly and vulgar looking paper,"[10] an attitude which seemed widespread. Still, perhaps the most attractive and imaginative offerings of the colonial newspaper were its display ads. That had always been true of patent medicine testimonials which pointed out how some man or woman had been saved from death's door by consuming that particular modern miracle. Doctor Hoofland's Celebrated German Bitters, for example, promised in the Montreal

Transcript (23 January, 1855) to cure jaundice, dyspepsia, constipation, heartburn, "fluttering of the heart," dimness of vision, yellowness of the skin and eyes, sudden flushes of heat, and "Constant Imaginings of Evil, and great Depression of Spirits." More slowly, other advertisers had learned the lesson of striking appeals, such as those retailers who announced in bold print "War Declared" and went on to note they meant a war on prices. By Confederation, large print, a wide variety and arrangement of type, white space, and illustrations appeared in big ads, many of which broke free from the column straitjacket. These ads were harbingers of the future transformation of the format and appearance of the newspaper.

The second offering of the press was a wide assortment of features designed to enlighten and amuse the populace. The colonial newspaper had something of the character of a magazine, perhaps another reason why the magazine press was so feeble. Even the first gazettes had given attention to literature. Joseph Howe's *Novascotian* won a certain local fame as a patron of the arts in the Halifax of the 1830s. At mid-century, book reviews were a common filler in Ontario newspapers when politics came to a brief standstill. But few of these papers could compete with the extensive coverage the francophone press gave the cultural scene of France and Europe generally. By this time, the colonial newspaper had begun to supply more light entertainment as a result of the successful example of the penny tri-weeklies of the late 1830s and early 1840s. Most newspapers carried a half column or so of humour and poetry on a regular basis, sometimes listed under the title "Miscellany" or "Extraits Divers." The big item was the feuilleton or serial novel. As early as 1827, the Kingston *Chronicle* had published installments of Walter Scott's *Life of Napoleon*. Again, though, the initiative of the penny tri-weeklies made the serial novel a must for the enterprising journalist. Some "good" books were serialized, such as Dickens' *Dombey and Son* and later *Uncle Tom's Cabin* by the *Globe*. But most novels were romances or adventure stories, escapist literature with titles like "La Vie de Corsaire" or "The Other Side: A Tale of Buttons." These foreign thrillers, for few were of native origin, popularized the stereotypes of heroism and villainy, of respectability and honour, of struggle and endurance and restraint, of a triumphant righteousness and a doomed evil which enriched the Victorian ethos. As much as all the sermons, tracts, teachings, and editorials, the serial novels helped to mould the social and moral ideals of the century. From another perspective, these novels were the progenitors of a type which would become so familiar to later generations, the bestseller, the "B" movie, and the radio and television soap operas — the staple of popular entertainment in the affluent society. The cultural importance of the much despised serial novel, then, was great, especially in a land where the book habit was not yet widespread.

Journalists took their duty to educate their readers as seriously as the need to entertain them. At first, this urge took a peculiar form. The early editor felt no compunction about filling the minds of the populace with whatever interested him. So the press of the 1820s and 1830s carried selections from philosophical and political tracts, disquisitions on family life or slavery, sermons old and new, and lectures on improved farming techniques. The Reform newspapers of French Québec were especially assiduous teachers of the thoughts of Voltaire, Diderot, and the encyclopédistes. Asahel Lewis included in his St. Thomas *Liberal* a good number of accounts of military warfare, especially from the career of Napoléon Bonaparte. James Fothergill used his newspaper, *The Palladium of British America*, to communicate large chunks of the result of twenty years labour in the natural history of Ontario. Over the years, W. L. Mackenzie and Joseph Howe carried in their weeklies a number of discussions of colonial life and society, the most famous being Howe's provincial "Rambles." All of which suggests the public had an indiscriminate hunger for knowledge, however trivial. Even accounts of Napoléon's battles might enliven the dull routine of life.

Things did change. Perhaps the influx of foreign publications made readers a trifle more discriminating. In any case, fewer editors by mid-century inflicted their eccentric interests upon the public. The features in the francophone press remained discernably more serious, indeed philosophical. Aside from the inevitable Voltaire, a reader might find, say, a discourse on Communism or a text from Proudhon (both appeared in *Le Canadien* for August and September of 1848). In particular, these newspapers carried extracts on matters of Catholic dogma and Catholic politics. Montréal's *La Minerve* published on 16 January, 1855 a learned discussion of "L'Immaculée Conception." By contrast, the features in the anglophone press were less learned, more practical or even frivolous. During the 1860s, for example, the Montreal *Witness* published columns of useful household hints for homemakers plus assorted homilies on the virtues of temperance for the whole family. On the lighter side were the discussions of contemporary fashions which had begun to appear in many a newspaper. Even more common were squibs of trivia about habits or events in exotic parts of the world. In the very respectable Montreal *Gazette* of 15 January, 1845 appeared items with titles like "Treatment of Women in Damascus" and "Turks at a European Ball in Egypt." Apparently, the anglophone journalist had decided to leave the cultivation of the higher life of mankind to other media.

Providing news was always an essential task of the colonial newspaper. The first gazettes were little more than newsletters. Later journals, especially newcomers, invariably promised to supply readers with copious amounts of information. What constituted news, though, changed dramatically over the years. Perhaps the signal change was in the immediacy of this news. Until the steamship and the telegraph, the colonial newspaper provided only a chronicle of the past. The editor depended upon the arrival of the mails and the ships to supply him with the needed copy, primarily other newspapers. In the 1830s, British news was still normally six weeks late, if not more given the state of trans-Atlantic communications. When winter isolated cities and towns in the interior, there was often a worrisome dearth of fresh material, both foreign and domestic. Only in the late 1840s and early 1850s did the newspaper begin to furnish what could properly be called a record of the present. For the telegraph companies entered the news business, dispensing to their clients up-to-date summaries of information about the colonies and the outside world. (Such an arrangement with a competitor so enraged the proprietor of the *New Brunswicker* that he apparently hired a man to cut the telegraph wires each morning.) A common offering of the new tri-weeklies and dailies was a half column or so of telegraphic news, a collection of terse snippets about happenings that would later be elaborated by extracts from the relevant newspapers. The bigger urban papers hired reporters who could be sent off to cover some major event like a murder trial or a train wreck. In any case, the daily's news columns made the paper unbeatable. The public had an apparently insatiable hunger for timely news about everything under the sun. ". . . The least deduction in quantity and quality of late news is now looked upon as an intolerable grievance," commented one journalist, "and the conductors of the daily press are treated with very little mercy, if they fail to cater exactly to meet the voracious appetites of their expectant patrons!"[11] The proprietor who fully exploited this fascination with news was bound to prosper.

But perhaps this was truer of English than French Canada. Francophone editors were much slower to respond to the demand for news. Indeed, they were notorious for their lack of interest in the quality of their news columns. One of the cardinal sins of the French-Canadian press, charged Hector Fabre, himself a journalist, was that "ils ne donnent pas assez de nouvelles, et surtout ils ne les donnent pas assez tôt." And he added, "le choix des etraits s'y fait trop souvent au hasard des ciseaux."[12] Rumour had it that even the prestige papers, like *La Minerve* or *Le Pays*, stole their news from their anglophone rivals. No wonder French Canadians purchased English papers to find out what was happening.

In the beginning, the great staple was foreign news, and the newspaper remained the colonist's window on the world. Canadians were, in their own fashion, a cosmopolitan people always intrigued by the doings great and small of the outside world. The lives of royalty, political and diplomatic crises, and wars were very good copy. During the 1790s and the 1800s, for instance, the colonial press supplied an incredible amount of news about the European conflict, sometimes to the exclusion of just about everything else. Much later, the London *Advertiser*, a newcomer in 1863, survived the first uncertain years of publication by satisfying the demand for copious reports about the American Civil War. More impressive, though, was the coverage the colonial press gave to the routine of life elsewhere. Francis Collins carried in his *Canadian Freeman* (1825-1834) of Toronto, whenever possible, a news column made up of clippings from Irish journals to keep his immigrant readers abreast of affairs in the homeland. Such special fare was common in all sectarian newspapers. By the 1850s, journalists had begun to hire part-time foreign correspondents to furnish regular accounts of events. *Le Courrier du Canada*, founded in 1857, employed one L.-A. de Puibusque, supposedly a good Catholic, who would not mislead the paper's ultramontane audience, to write about French affairs. At Confederation, the press, at least the anglophone newspapers, devoted a lot of space to the American scene, partly because of the availability of news. But not to the neglect of the rest of the colonist's world. British affairs were detailed. Europe received much attention, especially France in the francophone press. And a reader could find the occasional item on Asia, Africa, or South America culled from some foreign source. Much of this foreign news was abbreviated and trivial, often a series of one- or two-liners taken from the telegraphic reports or short paragraphs copied from other publications. But, whatever its flaws, the foreign coverage of the colonial newspaper was wide-ranging, sufficient to keep the Canadian public aware of affairs, even life, beyond the horizons of village and city.

This news, naturally, had to compete for space with more parochial reports. Intercolonial items were rarely numerous, even after the telegraph arrived. A newspaper with metropolitan pretentions, such as the St. John *Telegraph* during the 1860s, would specialize, though, in regular summaries of news from around the province. Moreover, urban newspapers, including the early gazettes, supplied at least a modicum of commercial news about ship movements or market prices as well as the occasional survey of business or the harvest. By Confederation, leading dailies like the Montreal *Gazette* or the Toronto *Globe* were famed for their coverage of the routine of economic life in and around their cities and, to a lesser extent, in the United States and overseas. In addition, notably after 1830, newspapers normally offered altogether a column or so, sometimes more of course, pertinent to the civic scene. Common here were notes on the comings and goings of the important, births and deaths, statistics on crime and illness, assorted pieces of local gossip — in all making a kind of community billboard. More detailed reports chronicled the organized public activities of the locale — thus, on 3 May, 1855, the Montreal *Transcript*, which like most popular newspapers was especially attentive to the local scene, recounted at length a special council meeting occasioned by some threatened strikes and carried the first annual report of the Protestant Industrial House of Refuge. Finally, contentious local issues, such as Toronto's esplanade controversy around 1860, or important happenings, say a severe fire or the opening of rail services, were always covered and often discussed. Even so, the coverage of the civic scene was not abundant, and given the space available that was hardly surprising, especially not in the party organs where foreign or political news usually had priority.

Increasingly noticeable over the years was an attempt to give news columns a certain sprightliness, a touch of humour, even a tinge of sensationalism. Naturally, the popular newspapers were the most aggressive manufacturers of this brand of news. Fairly common was to search through assorted sources for bits of unusual or entertaining trivia. Readers were regaled with tales of the birth of a two-headed cow, the passage of a comet, the nasty habits of African cannibals, or the exploits of a madman. On 16 August, 1844, the Toronto *Patriot* carried as filler on its third page a collection of short, racy items on mad dogs and hydrophobia in the Woodstock area, a game hunt in Cornwall, the arrest of a postmaster (courtesy of the "Detroit Adv."), and "Murder and Arson in the Indian Country" which noted troubles in the "Creek Nation." Another technique was to give special attention to disasters and crime. Earthquakes, fires, shipwrecks, epidemics, train accidents and so on readily found their way into news columns. Just as morbid were the accounts of murders, the resulting trials, and of course the executions. On 1 November, 1856, the Toronto *Globe*, for example, provided four and a half columns on the murder trial of George Brogdin, with the jury verdict supplied by telegraph. By the 1850s, again as a result of the example of the penny tri-weeklies, more and more urban newspapers had added a report of the proceedings of the police court that detailed the misdemeanors of petty criminals. So the underside of life received its due. Still, even the popular newspapers were only pale imitations of their supposed mentors, the cheap press of England and America. By its standards, the Canadian press was very proper.

That did not mean the colonial newspaper had sworn off sensationalism. Far from it. Rather the newspaper saved its distortions, its exposés, and its crusades for the coverage of the political arena. Politics flooded the news columns in the 1820s. That invasion began with copious reports of the assembly debates. Before long, though, editors published a wide assortment of partisan gossip, local and provincial. True, a momentary lull in political conflict might leave even the most zealous editor bereft of anything to report. True, the popular press eschewed the massive coverage of politics common in the party organs. But no newspaper remained for long aloof from the political battlefield.

And a surge of political excitement would drive everything else, including foreign reports, out of the news columns of the press. The editors freely mixed news and views. Not for them the cult of objectivity that would rule (in theory) the reporting practices of the mass press. Editors, proud of their partisan loyalties, convinced of the righteousness of their causes, played favourites. The practice of "party reporting" was widespread in the press, even amongst the country weeklies. Typically, a newspaper lavished attention on the actions of its friends, turning a blind eye to their peccadilloes, while mangling the speeches, distorting the aims, abusing the leaders, and trumpeting the sins of the enemy.

The public loved this biased reporting. With good reason. The newspaper's concentration upon political life had stripped bare the mystery which had surrounded government. No longer could the officials pretend politics was a game only for the genteel and the privileged. Readers now knew, or thought they knew, how government operated. As well, the press reports of parliamentary speeches brought the assembly into a much closer contact with the electorate. The assembly became, in truth, the representative of the popular will. Such a change enormously enhanced the power of the assembly, and thus defeated the intent of the colonial constitutions which had presumed the superior authority of governor, councils and officials. The way was paved for responsible government. Political news, better yet "party reporting," had undermined executive power and emphasized popular sovereignty. Was it surprising the ordinary citizen was satisfied?

The pride of the colonial newspaper was its opinion. That newspaper was, above all, an engine of controversy. Yet opinionated journalism had at first been very rare. The gazettes and their unofficial rivals were newsletters which usually avoided all but a timid commentary upon public affairs. Anything more might result in official displeasure. So early editors did not advocate any opinion — other than loyalty to the regime. Rather they made their newspapers a forum for all respectable opinions by publishing correspondence on the topic at issue. They, of course, could select the letters they preferred, so biasing the exchange. The founders of Le Canadien justified the launching of their newspaper with the charge that the Quebec Mercury had refused to publish letters which clashed with its proprietor's views. As well, editors or their friends did write under pseudonyms letters purportedly from concerned readers so as to ensure an airing of the right opinions. Certainly, that practice was much abused by the first Le Canadien (1806-1810). The early press was never a perfect forum of public opinion.

Initially, most of the controversies carried by the press were stilted, pointless affairs, perhaps concocted by the editor himself to fill space. The particular topic was usually very safe, the correspondents often circumspect, and the exchange normally a collection of elaborate insults. The letter-writers, invariably anonymous, used the occasion to display their literary skills, not necessarily their intelligence. But, in time, the controversies assumed a greater public significance. During the 1790s, both the Montreal *Gazette* and the Quebec *Herald*, albeit unofficial newspapers, used letters to express sympathy for the French Revolution and a desire to liberalize Québec's institutions. After 1805, the Quebec *Mercury* earned much notoriety by publishing letters which suggested Québec was too French, that the loyalties of its people lay with Napoléon, that the time had come to anglify this strange British possession. In retaliation, *Le Canadien* employed even more letters to defend the Québécois against these slanders and to popularize the assembly's challenge to officialdom. By the 1820s and 1830s, journals published regular columns of correspondence, such as the letters of "Algernon Sidney" on politics in the St. Thomas *Liberal*, or parliamentary analyses, such as the "Legislative Reviews" written by Joseph Howe and his friends for the *Novascotian*, or even open letters to the public urging some principle or revealing some abuse, W. L. Mackenzie's in the *Colonial Advocate* being especially notorious. Yet already correspondence had begun to wane as a vehicle of controversy. No longer did editors pretend neutrality; instead, if the issue was political, they selected letters that reflected their views. Sometimes, they trivialized correspondence columns by carrying letters designed to amuse readers. Or the editors allowed correspondence to express local grievances and special pleading, interesting yes but hardly germane to public debate. What supplanted correspondence was the editorial.

The first editorials had been very humble, little more than annotated tables of contents. Squirrelled away on the inside pages, under a timid masthead, these brief and occasional comments pointed out the interesting matter in the rest of the newspaper.[13] That practice remained common up to 1820, although by then an editorial column was a normal offering on the second page. During the next decade, however, the colonial press adopted the innovation of long editorials, pioneered by the British and American newspapers a generation earlier. These "leaders" were in fact essays, occasionally as much as two columns in length, wherein the editor could express his views on key issues. The leader was usually supplemented by short paragraphs on the lesser questions of the week. That innovation brought in its wake the heyday of opinionated journalism. True, all newspapers were not equally committed to vigorous debate. The Montreal *Transcript*, a popular newspaper, might not carry a leader, merely an assortment of brief comments, upstaged by a mass of ads and news. But contrast that with the editorial section in the Toronto *Globe*, a party organ, which might sport two or three long editorials, sometimes consuming the whole of page two. Certainly by Confederation, the editorial page was the heart of the colonial newspaper, the section upon which the journalist squandered so much energy and the reader doted so much attention.

The editor's world was a most peculiar place. For the editor in heat was a secular messiah bursting with a zeal to proselytize. His was the task eternal, to lead the people and the politicians in the ways of right-eousness. He readily assumed the garb of infallibility to preach the one true gospel, whatever that might be. Approaches did differ. As a rule, the francophone editor was more intellectual and literary, whereas the anglophone editor was more practical and concrete. The work of both, though, suggested a touch of paranoia. Surrounded by false prophets, that is rivals, the colonial editor was invariably pugnacious. So the quality of his comment did vary. At best, leaders were well-reasoned, vigorous disquisitions, spiced with wit and written with grace; at worst, leaders became pompous or turgid or abusive diatribes, more confused than perceptive. Even the famed George Brown had his bad days. Yet, on balance, the colonial editorial was a marvellous species of propaganda. The editor's purview might range over a myriad of topics: the nefarious intentions of the American Republic, the virtues of British institutions or the tyranny of British rule, the plight of the Pope or the Catholic threat to liberty, the evils of slavery but the merits of temper-ance, the need for immigration and railways, and on and on ad in-finitum. Still, the most space, the most energy was reserved for colonial politics. Time and again, the editor called the faithful to arms to defend the public weal against the villainous designs of the opposition. Such a call, of course, inspired the rival journalists to paroxysms of fury. And so a newspaper controversy often became a wonderful mélange of fact and fiction, principle and personality, reason and vitriol. There was, then, some justice to the charge that the editor always seemed intent upon creating a sensation to disturb the public mind. At times, even the journalists wearied of the constant fray: "The war rages across the whole line," cried a disgusted N. F. Davin (in the Nation, 24 Septem-ber, 1874), "and missiles of insult, slander, mendacity, and of moral ordure, are flung from side to side with blind fury." That aside, the most admired and feared editors were also the most furious, a man like Joseph Cauchon of Le Journal de Québec who was forever delivering sledgehammer blows to his political enemies. The colonists liked their politics served up raw and bloody.

The surge of opinionated journalism seemingly transformed the press into an agent of factional disorder. Each newspaper boasted its own unique blend of dogma and tradition. During the 1840s, a Toronto reader could choose from amongst the Patriot (Old Country, Church of England, and tory-minded), the Herald (Orange and conservative), the British Colonist (Scottish, Church of Scotland, and tory-minded), the Mirror (Irish, Catholic, and liberal), the Examiner (first liberal, later radical), the Globe (Scottish, Free Kirk, and liberal), and the popular Star. A decade later, Montréal played host, sometimes briefly, to its own strange congeries of papers: La Minerve (Catholic and conserva-tive), the extreme L'Avenir (anti-clerical and radical) soon superseded by the more moderate *Le Pays* (yet also anti-clerical and radical), the *Herald* (anglophone, commercial, and liberal) and the *Gazette* (equally anglophone and commercial but conservative), the *Witness* (evangelical and radical), the *Pilot* (Irish, popular, and ministerial), and the *Transcript* (popular and conservative). A contemporary anatomy of press opinion, Meikle's *Canadian Newspaper Directory* published in 1858, revealed that this anarchic profusion of religious, ethnic, and partisan "principles" was common throughout Québec and Ontario. Nor was the Maritimes any better. The collapse of the tory order left British America, albeit briefly, without an accepted or guiding body of ideas. Further complicating the picture was an invasion, via the press, of foreign ideas — from the British Isles, the United States, France, and for that matter Rome. Most important was the Canadian reality itself, a bubbling cauldron in which churned an unholy mixture of native-born and immigrant, Catholic and Protestant, Orange and Green, Anglican and Dissenter, Loyalist and American, etc., etc., all somehow represented in the press. No wonder public debate was constantly disturbed by old feuds and new doctrines, by the passions of race and religion.

The press was more than an instrument of faction, though. Newspapers had become the vehicles for certain distinct perspectives upon Canada's nature and destiny. Now these perspectives were not so much doctrines as loose collections of rhetoric, priorities, and ideals that informed the response to specific issues or policies. The weakest, and by Confederation especially feeble, was a radicalism born of tyranny at home and democracy abroad which looked forward to an egalitarian utopia. Supposedly, its greatest champion was William Lyon Mackenzie (the *Colonial Advocate*), but numbered in the radical camp were Patriote editors like Ludger Duvernay (*La Minerve*) and Reform voices like R. J. Parsons (the St. John's *Patriot*) during the 1830s, and Rouge democrats like L.-A. Dessaulles (*L'Avenir*) and Clear Grit spokesmen like William Macdougall (the *North American* of Toronto) during the 1850s, plus many lesser lights in the country press. The uneasy radical ally, a liberalism primarily of British origin touted the merits of a free community of self-reliant individuals. Its advocates were legion, men such as Joseph Howe (the *Novascotian*) in the Maritimes, Étienne Parent *(Le Canadien)* in Québec, or George Brown (the Toronto *Globe*) in Ontario, who sought to sweep away tory privilege and place power in the hands of the professional and business interests. The glory days of the liberal came to an end with the Reform era at mid-century, and thereafter he found himself battling a refurbished conservative enemy. Perhaps the ultimate victor was the conservatism that rose phoenix-like from tory ashes in the 1840s and 1850s to espouse the twin virtues of tradition and development. In conservative ranks were listed old Tories like William Pope (the Charlottetown *Islander*), old Reformers such as Joseph Cauchon (*Le Journal de Québec)* and James Beaty (the Toronto *Leader*), intransigent ultramontanes like Cyrille Boucher *(L'Ordre)*, and economic nationalists like the White brothers (first the Hamilton *Spectator*, and after Confederation the Montreal *Gazette*). A mixed group (few as famous as their rivals) but undeniably formidable because it was they who thrust the colonies toward union. In fact, by Confederation much of the press voiced an underlying satisfaction with colonial institutions and colonial ways.

That consensus was tied to the role of the press as the publicist of an emerging Victorian ethos. Granted the diversity of opinion on matters of race and religion, there was an astonishing uniformity to the social message of the newspapers. At the core of this message was the growth ethic, the conviction that more economic development was the key to progress. From the beginning of the century, journalists had rhapsodized about the Canadian potential in the smug belief the colonies would soon emulate the American achievement. The nineteenth, not the twentieth, was supposed to be "Canada's century." So the press idealized the progressive farmer, the busy workingman, and above all the entrepreneur. A journalist might sound the occasional note of alarm, notably the ultramontane editors who worried a lot about the advance of materialism. Yet even their francophone brethren were caught up in the railway craze of the 1850s, when journalists everywhere played the promoters' game by romanticizing the railway as civilization on wheels. Clustered about the growth ethic, of course, were a host of associated beliefs: an extraordinary commitment to self-improvement, the twin emphases upon individual self-reliance and social harmony, and a galloping puritanism. Time and again, the press boosted such social authorities as the church, the family, the school, and the courts and such social disciplines as morality, education, marriage, hard work, and respectability. Indeed, as early as the 1830s, newspapers had opened a campaign to order what now seemed a chaotic milieu with demands for free education, temperance and Sabbatarian laws, a police force and prison reform. Victorian Canada, so it would seem, was first born in the fertile minds of the journalists.

IV

This particular bias emphasized the close link that had grown up between the press and the establishment. Much ink had been spilled defending or explaining "the freedom of the press." Even the first publishers paid lip-service to the notion. Only after the emergence of an opinionated press, though, was the battle joined. A good number of the new breed of editors were, by instinct and persuasion, libertarians who resented any effort to muzzle their opinions. A few took a perverse pleasure in outraging convention and authority. But however admirable their ardour, they ran the risk of becoming martyrs to the cause. The more rabid editors sometimes suffered the rage of irate readers. In 1826, one of Mackenzie's diatribes against the Family Compact liberally spiced with bits of personal slander, led certain younger sons of official families to invade the offices of the *Colonial Advocate* and hurl its press into the Bay; ironically, the upshot was a trial which won Mackenzie £ 625 in damages, saving him from a bankruptcy that would likely have closed down his newspaper. Less happy was the lot of Henry Winton, proprietor of the St. John's *Public Ledger:* a tory whose opinions incensed local Irish Catholics, he was set upon by a gang of toughs who cut off his ears to teach him a lesson.

The chief enemy of a free press, of course, remained the tory official. In 1810, Governor Craig had his agents raid the offices of the rambunctious *Le Canadien*, seizing its press and all papers on the premises. Then, once a confession had been extracted from the hapless printer, Craig had imprisoned on charges of treason Pierre Bédard, other proprietors of the paper, plus some prominent assemblymen. If nothing later on quite compared with Craig's "reign of terror," there were numerous other "outrages," as the Reformers were wont to call them. Three times Ludger Duvernay was imprisoned for libel. Francis Collins went to jail for calling Attorney-General Robinson, among other things, a "native malignancy." R. J. Parsons of the St. John's *Patriot* so infuriated Chief Justice Boulton that, all alone, he prosecuted and judged the editor, sentencing the poor man to pay a fine and to spend three months in jail. Joseph Howe only escaped ruin because a jury, against the clear intent of the law, acquitted him of charges of criminal libel. Accused of "seditious scheming" in 1838, Étienne Parent languished in prison for four months, a sojourn which left him almost deaf thereafter. Parent's arrest was a result of the Rebellions, and the tory determination to stamp out the Reform menace once and for all. The Reform press in Québec and Ontario was decimated. But it was a hollow victory. The public would no longer tolerate the authoritarian rigour of an earlier day. In particular, as Howe's trial, among others, demonstrated, juries were not likely to discharge their duty under law in any clash between the press and officialdom.

The libertarian victory did firmly establish the notion of freedom of the press in Canada's unwritten constitution. The victory was also an admission that the principle of private enterprise applied to the conduct of journalism. The newspaper produced a special commodity, a particular image of life, in what amounted to a self-regulating marketplace of ideas. Anyone was free to launch his own journal to express his distress or forward his panacea. No longer need the proprietor fear that official action would hobble his right to publish. Indeed, the libertarian victory so hamstrung government that the hallowed freedom often became licence. No matter. The public, the consumers, would decide via their choices what was legitimate. This was justified by a panoply of liberal assumptions. "Remember, that wherever the Press is not free the people are poor abject degraded slaves," commented W. L. Mackenzie (in the *Colonial Advocate*, 26 January, 1832), "that the Press is the life, the safeguard, the very heart's blood of a free country; the test of its worth, its happiness, its civilization. . . ." For the very clash of ideas would enable the citizenry to discover Truth. Everyman could read everything to come to his own conception of what was right and proper. Thus, the individual became the final arbiter of his own destiny. The notion of freedom of the press had been inextricably linked to the notion of popular sovereignty. The naive yet splendid trust in the efficacy of unrestrained debate and the rationality of the common man was eventually sanctified by John Stuart Mill's famous essay "On Liberty," which was really a sophisticated elaboration of beliefs already commonplace throughout the British and American worlds. Repeatedly, his line of argument would be resurrected to defend the Canadian media against some effort to impose public controls upon their actions.

Appearances aside, however, the libertarian victory did not transform the colonial press into a free press. By definition, a free press must be an autonomous institution, must enjoy a degree of independence from the influence of other centres of power in the community. That independence the press lacked, whatever the promise implicit in the struggles of the 1820s and 1830s. Admittedly, the boasted independence of these first journals of opinion had often been illusory. All claimed some kind of connection, and many relied upon a patron. By and large, the opinions of the Tory newspapers were the most closely controlled. Leading Tory newspapers like the Toronto *Patriot*, the Montreal *Gazette*, *L'Ami du Peuple*, and the St. John's *Public Ledger* constituted the voices of the ruling authorities, or rather of the factions within these circles. Partly, the acquiescence of the Tory editor grew out of a belief in the legitimacy of the crumbling authoritarian order he defended. Equally significant was the power of the establishments, which prevented their journalists from attaining a lasting independence. Not so, or not as much, the Reform press. Indeed, there was a rugged honesty about the rhetoric of that press. Journalists like Étienne Parent, William Lyon Mackenzie, or Joseph Howe were never just party propagandists. Sometimes, their maverick views distressed or angered political friends, John Neilson, owner of the Quebec *Gazette*, actually broke with his one-time colleague, L.-J. Papineau, and opened a campaign against the rebellious course of the parti canadien in 1836. Again, in part, this independence grew out of conviction, out of a libertarian ardour. But equally important was the fact that the Reform oppositions were loose coalitions which lacked the will and the resources to effectively discipline their publicists. These publicists were often party leaders in their own right.

The emerging tradition of press independence was stillborn, unfortunately. Perhaps the conclusion of the struggle against officialdom lessened the libertarian ardour of the profession. The enemy defeated, the journalists were no longer sensitive to the key issue of independence. In any case, soon after the Rebellions, the ambitious and the powerful established a stranglehold on the press in order to manipulate the new god of public opinion the press had awakened. Politicians led the way, and remained the most obvious masters of the press, though they were followed by Catholic churchmen and the occasional businessman. Their initiatives maintained the clutter of organs which came to dominate the Canadian scene in city and town. In 1838, Robert Baldwin approved the establishment of the Toronto *Examiner* to rally the demoralized Reformers behind the new panacea of responsible government. In 1842, L.-H. Lafontaine recalled Ludger Duvernay from his exile in the United States to publish a reborn *La Minerve*. In 1844, Joseph Howe and William Annand founded the Halifax *Chronicle* to provide Nova Scotian Reformers with a metropolitan organ (to which Conservatives soon replied with the Halifax *British Colonist*). Bishop Bourget of Montréal in 1850 sponsored the *True Witness and Catholic Chronicle* to defend the Irish Catholics against the abuse of the Anglo-Protestant press. Eight years later, the clergy of the diocese of Québec supplied the funds for *Le Courrier du Canada*, designed to combat the opinions of the Rouge press. In 1857, the Grand Trunk Railway, a heavy consumer of public funds, had itself advanced monies to keep the Toronto *Daily Colonist* afloat as a Conservative organ. During the early 1870s, Hugh Allan apparently owned the Montreal *Gazette* and held a loan on *La Minerve*, the two Conservative government organs, both of which by chance supported his railway schemes.

These masters made sure their charges remained reliable. After 1855 apparently, John A. Macdonald corresponded regularly with the publishers of the Montreal *Gazette* on matters of party policy. Luther Holton, a Québec Liberal, kept a close watch over the editorials of the Montreal *Herald*, as did Leonard Tilley, the Liberal premier of New Brunswick, in the case of the St. John *News*. Both newspapers were known as the personal mouthpieces of these gentlemen. At first, an ecclesiastical censor supervised the content of *Le Nouveau Monde*, an ultramontane paper founded in Montréal in 1867. Charles Tupper, so he later claimed, wrote many of the leaders for the Halifax *British Colonist* between 1855 and 1870. Jonathon McCully, a Liberal leader in Nova Scotia's legislative council, was the editor of the Halifax *Chronicle* in the six years prior to 1864. A number of politicians were themselves proprietors of leading newspapers: Joseph Cauchon of *Le Journal de Québec*, T. W. Anglin of the St. John *Freeman*, Edward Whelan of the Charlottetown *Examiner*, and, of course, George Brown of the *Globe*. Brown was especially fortunate, since he could count upon the excellent services of brother Gordon when otherwise engaged in the affairs of parliament.

By and large, the profession submitted quietly to this yoke. True,

editors or proprietors were wont to grumble about the constant badger-
ing of their masters, on occasion breaking free out of spite or over a
principle. For instance, the *Acadian Recorder* of Halifax, a Conservative organ, split away from Tupper in 1864, supposedly because it
opposed Confederation. But a pure, lasting independence was very,
very rare. George Sheppard, perhaps the most accomplished of the
pre-Confederation editors in the two Canadas, at one time declared that
it was the duty of the journalist to bow to the collective wisdom of his
party. Indeed, the greatest proprietor of them all, George Brown, felt
bound by the demands of a party he had fathered. Only the Montreal
Witness among the leading dailies was free of any entanglements,
though John Dougall's radical and anti-clerical sympathies usually
placed the newspaper in the Rouge camp.

Conviction, fear, and greed dictated submission. The profession, be-
devilled by financial insecurity and factional loyalties, lacked the for-
titude to resist. The devoutly Catholic George Clerk rarely undertook a
new line in the *True Witness* without the approval of Bourget. Rollo
Campbell of the Montreal *Pilot* once boldly announced his newspaper
was the trusted organ of the Conservative government of the day. If
loyalty did not suffice, then the master could always punish an intract-
able maverick. When in 1844 *L'Aurore des Canadas*, a lukewarm sup-
porter of the Reform cause, had the temerity to back its opponents,
Lafontaine's cronies persuaded partisans to cancel their subscriptions,
resulting in the paper's disappearance eighteen months later. Macdonald sponsored the *Daily Atlas* in 1858 to wreck the *Daily Colonist*
of Toronto for its criticism of the government, a move that resulted in
the amalgamation of the two newspapers under a reliable management.
Besides, acquiescence could be so lucrative. Some newspapers could
not have lasted without subventions from patrons. The party in office
was expected to release a stream of money to its press friends. A parliamentary inquiry revealed that by 1862 the Conservative government
of the two Canadas was spending well over $100,000 a year to feed an
ever-hungry gaggle of proprietors. One stalwart, William Gillespy of
the Hamilton *Spectator*, earned around $15,000 in four years for as-
sorted services to the government. The prize plum, the Queen's printer-
ship, could yield such sums annually to the happy journalists. As well,
the politician was expected to look after the retirement of the faithful.
Rollo Campbell, who closed the *Pilot* down when the Conservatives fell
from power in 1862, reappeared on government pay lists in 1865 as a
Customs officer (his friends having regained office). That same year,
Evariste Gélinas, who had exhausted himself as an editor of *La
Minerve*, obtained a sinecure in the Department of Militia. By Confederation, then, a dizzying variety of bonds, tangible and intangible,
linked the press to the powerful.

V

The press was Canada's first mature mode of communication, its messages reaching many people.[14] Not all of the people, though: the colonial press was never a mass medium. The wave of popularization after the mid-1830s may have given birth to the penny paper and modified an earlier pattern of journalism, but it had receded before substantially altering the bourgeois nature of the press. Indeed, this phenomenon had only a modest impact upon the francophone newspapers which remained extraordinarily highbrow in tone and content. And the Victorianism of the mid-century had actually strengthened the urge toward respectability amongst anglophone newspapers, including the popular alternative. So the colonial newspaper continued to chronicle and discuss "the little happenings of bourgeois society."[15] No more than a few journals really tried for long to cater to the tastes of the lower orders.

Secondly, although the influence of the tri-weeklies and the dailies did extend over the countryside, these newspapers rarely enjoyed a large circulation and their penetration of the public varied widely from province to province. Only two dailies, first the Toronto *Globe* and later the Montreal *Witness*, reached a mass audience. The economics of journalism ensured that most newspapers would continue to depend upon the patronage of small and particular constituencies. Besides, while Ontario could boast a rich variety of newspapers, French Québec supported a sparse collection of urban dailies and country weeklies which could never match the public significance of their anglophone brethren.[16]

Finally, the influence the newspaper might exercise was limited by the unequal and imperfect level of literacy amongst the adult population. The first Dominion census, in 1871, revealed that around 80% of people over twenty years of age claimed the ability to read. The statistic, in fact, was misleading. The literate population included just over 90% of Ontario's adults but barely 50% of Québec's francophone adults. Even the illiterate, of course, might well be subject to the indirect influence of a newspaper. There was a fair chance a literate relative or friend would communicate the substance, if not the contents, of a newspaper to the less skilled. And not just at home but after church, at work, or perhaps in the tavern, which as far back as the 1820s earned a reputation as a reading room cum public forum. On the other hand, much of the supposedly literate population had only an imperfect ability to read, obviously an obstacle to the understanding of all but the most simple printed thoughts. A medium made up of a host of bourgeois journals of opinion, speaking to a series of fragmented audiences that included readers whose comprehension varied enormously, could never be the instrument of mass communication.[17]

Even granted these limitations, however, the colonial press was everywhere of some importance. Its significance derived from the very nature of an open society wherein debate played so central a part. The clutter of newspapers encouraged the vigorous expression of divergent viewpoints. Thus, with eight competing tri-weeklies, Halifax in 1864 amply satisfied the libertarian ideal of intellectual diversity. Each newspaper had a distinctive personality, noticeable in its coverage of the news and its treatment of the issues.[18] Other cities were almost as fortunate, boasting sufficient newspapers to give voice to a wide range of opinions, albeit always bourgeois. In addition, if not a regular item in the homes of the poor, newspapers entered the homes of businessmen, professionals, artisans, and farmers in large numbers. Circumstantial evidence suggests that by Confederation many urban readers took more than one journal, at least a tri-weekly or daily plus a sectarian newspaper or a "class" weekly. Newsworthy papers like the Toronto Globe circulated in homes no matter what their political loyalties. The Globe's presence in Conservative households, in fact, was a source of much dissatisfaction to John A. Macdonald and his cronies, enough to force the party to finance an equally newsworthy and aggressive Mail in 1872. A similar kind of situation existed in Montréal where anglophone dailies, even the anti-Catholic Witness, found many francophone readers. What this meant was that competing opinions did reach people, at least in and around the cities. J. S. Mill's vision of public debate had some substance in colonial Canada.

It follows that the journalists constituted Canada's closest equivalent to a national intelligentsia, in other words a body of people whose stock in trade was ideas. These ideas may have originated with others, especially once the politicians had disciplined the press, but the fact remains the journalist was unsurpassed as a salesman of culture. Early on, at least in English Canada, the journalists had challenged (in effect, if not always intentionally) the social authority of the clergy. Not quite in French Canada, where the low level of literacy amongst the rural population insulated priestly power from the threat of the press. As it was, the social authority of the priest received a few jolts during the 1850s from the radical journalists in the Rouge camp. Professional rivalry had much to do with the cool relations between journalists and clergymen during the nineteenth century. Certainly, the clergy's recognition that the press was as mighty as the pulpit inspired clerical criticism of journalism, in the hope its power would not be used to vitiate the Christian presence in society. The aggressive denunciations of "la mauvaise presse" by the Catholic episcopacy of Québec, sometimes complete with an ecclesiastical ban on a particular newspaper (such as the Montreal Witness in 1875), were the more extreme manifestations of the clergy's determination to remain the moral censor of the country. Everywhere, the cleric had to live with the uneasy reality that a potent influence upon the minds of the faithful was the secular voice of the press.

Likewise, the politician found his brief dominion over public debate undone. The emergence of a partisan press had, initially, enhanced the import of the politician's rhetoric by focussing attention upon the assembly. But not for long: the parliamentary speech could not compare with the lead editorial as a tool of controversy and persuasion. Besides, once the battle over responsible government was over, members of parliament devoted more and more time to the mundane details of running the provinces. By the 1870s, the great questions of the day were first considered in the press, only afterwards, if at all, in parliament. It was, for example, Québec's journalists who vigorously debated the crucial issue of state and church in that decade, not the province's parliamentarians whose minds were on roads, railways, patronage, and power. There was some merit to Goldwin Smith's observation "that the power of journalism, great as it is, is still on the increase. The real debate has been transferred from assemblies, deliberative no longer, to the press, and the assembly does little more than record the conclusion."[19]

Together, the bourgeois readership of the newspaper and the cultural significance of the journalist made the press an agency of legitimation. That awkward term "legitimation" refers to the process whereby ideas receive the imprimatur necessary to inform private behaviour and public policy. Put another way, the process denotes the conversion of the novel into the orthodox. The press, in effect, created public opinion, the force which came to justify political authority throughout Canada. This act of creation involved first the articulation of ideas. The colonial press, or rather its masters, decided what it would reflect in the surrounding society, so giving substance to hopes and fears which hitherto had only a slight public significance. Late eighteenth century Canada was filled with social tensions. But these had a limited impact upon public policy until the new journals of opinion expressed the assorted grievances within each colony. What the press articulated it also simplified. However these ideas might arise, the press transformed them into stereotypes, symbols and slogans, which could be readily consumed by the public. After the mid-1820s, Ontario's Reform newspapers (led by Mackenzie's *Colonial Advocate*) manufactured the "Family Compact," a useful myth that suggested an oligarchy which had grasped unto itself power and privilege.[20] Lastly, the press propagandized ideas, the very fact of publicity soon turning the unfamiliar into the commonplace. From the early 1850s, first the Toronto *Globe* and soon its Liberal allies made popular both representation by population and northwest expansion, as means whereby Ontario might realize its destiny. By the next decade, even Conservative politicians felt constrained to pay lip-service to these notions.

Worth emphasizing, of course, is the fact that the press created many public opinions. Newspapers reinforced the innumerable "limited identities"[21] that studded the social landscape. That became very clear during the course of the Confederation debates. Each paper carefully linked the issue of union to local interests. The St. John *News* believed union would convert its city into the Manchester of Canada, the industrial capital of a vast agricultural hinterland. *La Minerve* assumed Montréal would reign supreme as the commercial entrepôt of the future nation, able to control and tithe all trade in and out of Canada. By contrast, the *Chronicle* feared Halifax's commerce would be strapped by the workings of a new national tariff. The Montreal *Herald* argued that its metropolis would prosper best in a closer economic accord with the United States, an accord endangered by the effort to organize a single Canadian economy. Every newspaper boosted the ambitions and denounced the enemies of its locale. The cities and towns were still island communities, set off from their neighbours by a pride of place as well as by distance.

Further, the colonial newspaper championed the cause of its province. The London *Free Press* foresaw a "new nationality" in which progressive Ontario would flourish as the empire province. The Halifax *British Colonist* dreamed of a Nova Scotia that would wax powerful as the gateway to an enormous transcontinental state. On the other hand, the Quebec *Mercury* worried that in any Confederation the distinct ways and separate ambitions of Québec would be trampled underfoot by an arrogant Ontario. *L'Union Nationale* set against the symbol of a "new nationality" the spectre of anglicization, hoping the Québécois might find their own fatherland in separation rather than join someone else's in union. The assorted provincialisms were, if anything, emphasized by the Confederation debates.

Most important, the comment, the news, even the entertainment of the colonial newspaper still nourished the psychological isolation of the various races and creeds. Note the example of Patrick Boyle's Toronto weekly, the *Irish Canadian*. One issue of the paper (7 April, 1869) furnished three letters on Irish Fenianism, a discussion of the "Amnesty Movement" in Ireland, a poem entitled "My Munster Mary" and an excerpt of the serial novel "Con Cregan: The Irish Gil Blas." Always, the paper doted attention on the doings of the Irish Catholic community and the Roman Catholic church in Ontario. Beyond this, the *Irish Canadian* sang the praises of Irish traditions and Catholic values, sounded the grievances of the much-abused minority, attacked the Orange and Scottish enemy, and demanded social and religious equality for all. The *Irish Canadian*, of course, was a sectarian weekly. But its message was no more than an extreme expression of what was normal in the press. *La Minerve* and *Le Pays*, however different their politics, not only cultivated the notion of French-Canadian superiority, but championed "la survivance," constantly on guard against Protestant or

English schemes that might threaten the French fact. Even the Toronto *Globe*, the first mass circulation daily, perpetuated beyond Confederation the closed world of its very British and Protestant readers, by incorporating their values and prejudices in an aggressive nationalism that demanded conformity from other races and creeds. The colonial newspaper communicated to its followers a beleaguered state of mind, a sense of worth, and peril, plus a crusading zeal, all of which emphasized the turbulence of life in what contemporaries called Canada's "mixed community."

Even so, the press did work in a variety of ways on behalf of a wider sense of brotherhood. The newspaper had soon become the advocate of the bourgeois citizenry. Admittedly, a fully developed middle class did not emerge until the post-Confederation era, and then only in the cities and towns of the new Dominion. But long before then, an assortment of lawyers, merchants, storekeepers, yeoman farmers, and the like had taken command of the detail of Canadian life. The journalists, emphatically bourgeois themselves, legitimated this emerging class, its ideals and its dominance. What, after all, was the cry of popular government about, a cry so loud in the Reform press, if not the handing over of political authority in the provinces and the towns to the bourgeoisie? Once the victory of responsible government assured these citizens political pre-eminence, the francophone radicals in the Rouge press went on to demand the abolition of seigneurial tenure, a free nonsectarian education, and the end of the tithe, all to liberate the rural population according to the social presumptions of an advancing bourgeois order. If their success was limited by clerical resistance and rural indifference, in Ontario the bourgeois journalist and his master had their way. Indeed, everywhere in English Canada, the cult of the entrepreneur was predominant by Confederation — and not just in business circles, but in politics and the professions as well. Overall, the colonial press had helped to make bourgeois ways, then better termed the Victorian ethos, a leading force especially at the top of society. Hence, the emergence in the cities of local elites agreed upon their values and ambitions. Hence also, the dynamism of an age confident of its virtue, eager to get on with the business of development.

Likewise, the press had sponsored a national idea which eventually bound together the disparate interests in a single political and economic structure. This effect dated from the first decades of the century, when the new focus of the press upon colonial affairs began the slow process whereby people come to identify with their land of residence. However great his interest in the outside world, the Canadian was involved by his newspaper in the life of his society. Even the Tory organs of the 1820s and 1830s assisted — they nationalized the British connection by emphasizing that the colonies were the outposts of British civilization, menaced by republican hordes to the south and disgruntled demagogues at home. This timid parochialism was strengthened during the 1830s and 1840s as the press fashioned a distinctive style of thought, manifested in the various perspectives the newspapers brought to bear upon public affairs. The victorious liberalism of these decades was tailored to suit the particular needs of the colonial milieu. Perhaps the demise of the radical press had something to do with the fact that neither Rouge nor Grit journalists could free their creeds from the charge of being French or American, unwelcome imports of the alien doctrine of democratic republicanism? After 1850, leading tri-weeklies and dailies often flirted with the notion of a Kingdom of the North, albeit still linked to the mother country. Such a heady vision eventually found expression in the rhetoric of pro-Confederate newspapers as dissimilar as the Toronto *Globe*, *La Minerve*, and Halifax's *British Colonist*. The vigour of anti-union sentiment in the press of Québec and the Maritimes, of course, demonstrated the national idea was still a suspicious novelty to many colonists. But a decade after Confederation, the newspapers had closed ranks behind the first panCanadian nationalism, that unionist credo which matured during the mid-1860s. Although there would be some backsliding and much disillusionment in the years ahead, the press had added the national idea to the pantheon of principles, including liberty, private property, and British connection, which constituted the Canadian orthodoxy.

The outstanding effect of the colonial press, though, was the exaltation of politics. Politics, like religion, was one of the great passions of the nineteenth century. Not just because of its intrinsic significance: playing politics was, in fact, a great game that fascinated both high and low, especially around election time. The journalists had awakened and fueled the public enthusiasm for politics. The news columns chronicled in excessive detail the course of politics for its eager fans. The editorial page persuaded an assortment of readers that their interests depended upon the result of conflicts in the political arena. In the two decades after 1850, Timothy Anglin's St. John *Freeman* worked to assure (apparently with some success) the Irish Catholic community of New Brunswick its grievances could only be redressed by the rule of right-thinking liberals. During the early 1860s, William Pope's Charlottetown *Islander* called upon the Protestant majority to unite behind the Conservative government to forestall Romish aggression. The party organs, in particular, linked the grievances and ambitions of the locale to the higher politics of the provincial capitals. *La Minerve* and the Montreal *Gazette* saw Cartier's Bleus and Macdonald's Conservatives as the political instruments of Montréal's merchant princes. Brown's *Globe*, not surprisingly, denounced the same politicians as tools of the Bank of Montreal and the Grand Trunk Railway, therefore hostile to the emerging commercial empire of Toronto.

Even though the real importance of government had declined after the mid-century, the constant manufacture of villains and heroes, of alarms and plots, had perpetuated the identification of the hopes and fears of the ordinary elector with the events transpiring in the political arena. "Strong food has created strong appetite," claimed T. C. Patterson of the Toronto *Mail*. "If I was respectable the people called me dull, if literary and argumentative I was heavy. A dish spiced with personalities, on the other hand, I was not slow in finding from the exchanges exactly suited the palates of the public."[22] For, although the elector might boast allegiance to abstract principles, his interest was engaged by the doings of the greats in politics like Macdonald or Cartier and their followers in the towns and cities of the land. So John Willison, a famous editor of a later age, recalled in his *Reminiscences* the tumultuous atmosphere of his first political meeting in 1872, at a place called Varna in the Ontario backwoods. There, a Conservative newcomer Thomas Greenway, the old Liberal chieftain Malcolm Cameron, and the maverick E. B. Wood (or "Big Thunder") regaled for hours an audience of locals, provoking flurries of boos and cheers whenever someone scored a debating point. (From that moment, Willison dated his own love of political debate.) The meeting had all the flavour of a modern hockey match. Indeed, politics was the prime form of public entertainment, combining the qualities of excitement and drama and pathos now a part of the sports scene. That trite phrase popular with present-day sports announcers, "the agony of defeat and the ecstasy of victory," is an apt description of the emotional fervour surrounding political controversy. In sum, the news and views of the press, especially its focus upon personalities, gave substance to the partisan loyalties which by the 1870s had come to discipline the voting habits of the populace. This achievement alone demonstrated the importance of the press.

The colonial press had served to reinforce the values and strengthen the institutions of an emerging Victorian Canada. The press was only one factor in the social equation, of course. Life was still regulated by a web of custom, some of which had roots in the far past. That was especially true of rural Québec where the illiteracy of much of the francophone population protected folkways. Custom reigned throughout a good deal of English Canada as well, at the bottom end of society, amongst Irish labourers, farmers, and the artisans. The press acted more on the upper reaches of Canadian life, among the bourgeois citizenry of the towns who were inveterate readers. Even here, the press really seconded the efforts of the makers of Victorian Canada, a fact signified by the control they exercised over its opinions. Newspapers assisted, they did not inspire or even determine, the rise of the mixed community, or in other words the clerics and businessmen and lawyers who led the ethnic garrisons and the many towns of Canada. The elaboration of a stylized political warfare, if impossible without the press, owed as much to the professional politicians who had purchased the editors. The political parties, though dependent upon the partisan loyalities the press nurtured, were kept alive by the promise of office and the skill of their chieftains as well as the cement of principle. In general, other social institutions, notably the church and the family, enjoyed a much greater authority over private behaviour than the press. The colonial newspaper was too eccentric, too subservient, and too restricted a medium to act as the premier agency of social control.

Notes:

[1] "Address of the Honourable Chief Justice Robinson; On Passing Sentence of Death upon Samuel Lount and Peter Matthews" (29 March 1838), Library of the Law Society of Upper Canada. For a brief but excellent exposition of the nature and significance of Robinson's address see Kenneth McNaught, "Political Trials and the Canadian Political Tradition," in M. L. Friedland, editor, Courts and Trials: A Multidisciplinary Approach (Toronto: University of Toronto Press, 1975), especially pp. 141-143.

[2] Cited in H. Pearson Gundy, Early Printers and Printing in Canada (Toronto: The Bibliographical Society of Canada, 1957), p.19. Simcoe eventually got his printer, one Louis Roy from Montréal. Unfortunately, Roy soon proved inadequate — perhaps because, as Lady Simcoe put it, he "cannot write good English." (21)

[3] S. Moodie, Mark Hurdlestone, The Gold Worshipper (London 1853), I, xx-xxii as cited in J. J. Talman, "Three Scottish-Canadian Newspaper Editor Poets," Canadian Historical Review, 28, 1947, p. 166.

[4] Such as the Montreal Transcript (1836-1865), St. John News (1839-1884), Halifax Herald (1840-1848?) and Post (1840-1848?), and the Toronto Star (1840-1846).

[5] For instance, among the Irish Catholic papers: Montréal's True Witness and Catholic Chronicle (1850-1910), Halifax Catholic (1854-1857), Toronto's Catholic Citizen (1854-1858), St. John's Record (1861-1863), Charlottetown Vindicator (1862-1864), and the Irish Canadian (1863-1901) of Toronto. And among ultramontane papers: Montréal's Les Mélanges Religieux (1841-1852), Le Courrier du Canada (1857-1901) of Québec City, Montréal's L'Ordre (1858-1861), when lost to the Liberals), Le Journal des Trois-Rivières (1865-1891), and Montréal's Le Nouveau Monde (1867-1881, when lost to the Conservatives).

[6] Quote cited in J. M. S. Careless, Brown of the Globe, v. 2: Statesman of Confederation 1860-1880 (Toronto: Macmillan of Canada, 1963). p. 112.

[7] "The Press of Ontario. By a Member of the Fourth Estate," New Dominion Monthly (February, 1872), p. 66.

[8] Helen Elliot, editor, Fate, Hope and Editorials 1862-1873 (Ottawa: Canadian Library Association, 1967), p. 114.

[9] Moodie, Mark Hurdlestone, The Gold Worshipper, I, xx-xxii cited in Talman, "Three Scottish-Canadian Newspaper Editor Poets," p. 166.

[10] The Daily Newspaper: The History of Its Production and Distribution (Montréal: John Dougall and Son, 1878), p. 18.

[11] The News of the World, 24 March 1855 (the weekly edition of Toronto's daily Colonist) cited in J. J. Talman, "The Newspaper Press of Canada West, 1850-60," Transactions of the Royal Society of Canada, series 3, 33, 1939, section 2, p. 149.

[12] Quoted in A. Beaulieu and J. Hamelin, La Presse Québécoise des origines à nos jours 2: 1860-1879 (Québec: Les Presses de l'Universite Laval, 1975), p. 97.

[13] For example, in the Halifax Gazette of 27 March, 1798, the proprietor included on page three under the heading "Halifax: March 27" some brief paragraphs which pointed out the arrival of a British warship with some interesting news — and mentioned what was extracted — but refrained from making any comment on the recent peace proposals, noted the report of the recent death of John Wilkes with some mildly disparaging observations on the life of this notorious libertarian, and commented happily upon the renewed unity of the British people in the face of a threatened French invasion.

[14] This kind of a judgement is always subjective. I have chosen an index based upon the circulation of all journals (newspapers and periodicals) from Rowell's American Newspaper Directory for 1873 and the number of families resident in Canada according to the census of 1871. Newspapers were consumed by families, rather than by one reader. Of course, this is a very rough index. Here are the number of journals per

family: Canada (1.08), Ontario (1.29), Québec (.95), New Brunswick (1.05), and Nova Scotia (.58). It is, in fact, quite likely that there were more journals in existence in 1873 than found their way into the directory.

[15] I have taken that phrase from a diatribe of the second congress of the Third International, cited in Owen Chadwick's *The Secularization of the European Mind in the Nineteenth Century* (Cambridge: Cambridge University Press, 1975), p. 42.

[16] Compare the anglophone and francophone newspapers (not all journals, note, only the newspapers) in Québec listed in Rowell's *American Newspaper Directory* for 1873. Admittedly, the francophone papers were probably underrepresented, but not sufficiently to deny the implication of the figures. There were some sixteen francophone newspapers with a combined circulation of 54,000 copies and twenty-six anglophone newspapers with a combined circulation of 83,000.

[17] There are difficulties with any definition of mass communication. I employ a very flexible definition, which comprehends a wide variety of communication experiences. By "mass communication," I mean the regular transmission of a uniform message by a small group of communicators to a large, anonymous, and diversified public.

[18] Here is a brief anatomy of the Halifax press for June and July of 1864. The Conservative *British Colonist* and the Liberal *Morning Chronicle* were the party organs (each appearing on Tuesday, Thursday, and Saturday), no doubt intended as well for a provincial audience, which gave copious coverage to political affairs. The Liberal *Citizen* and the Conservative *Acadian Recorder* were highly partisan, but more local and not offical organs. The *Morning Journal*, to the neglect of local and political matter, specialized in the Civil War, reporting and commenting from an unvarnished Southern viewpoint. Likewise, the *Evening Express* avoided extreme partisanship (though sympathetic to Tupper's Conservative government) and favoured the South, but offered a more varied fare. Their rival was the *Morning Sun* (again worth noting, perhaps, that these three papers appeared on Monday, Wednesday, and Friday), a pro-Northern advocate but also a chronicler of the local scene. Finally, the *Reporter* was Halifax's popular alternative, definitely specializing in local affairs but with much news and entertainment. It did have a large editorial section, with a ministerial and Southern bias but also a wide scope that took in provincial politics, foreign affairs, science and development, life and society.

[19] "The Press Banquet to Mr. Goldwin Smith, M.A.," *Rose-Belford's Canadian Monthly*, 7 (July-December 1881), p. 104.

[20] See G. Patterson, "An enduring Canadian myth: Responsible Government and the Family Compact," *Journal of Canadian Studies*, 12, Spring 1977, pp. 3-16.

[21] For some discussion of this phenomenon, see J. M. S. Careless, " 'Limited Identities' in Canada," *Canadian Historical Review*, 50, 1969, pp. 1-10.

[22] Cited in G. P. de T. Glazebrook, *The Story of Toronto* (Toronto: University of Toronto Press, 1971), p. 153.

II
The Golden Age of The Press

In 1889, the editors of the Toronto *Telegram* published a pamphlet in praise of the success of their newcomer to the ranks of the press. Therein, some anonymous soul appended a few notes on the awesome significance (as he saw it) of newspapers. One grand sentence acclaimed the press "the lungs of civilization, inhaling current history, science, art, politics, theology, literature and social problems, and assimilating them to the people from the highest to the lowest."[1] Exaggerated perhaps, but also prophetic. Before long, the press had become an instrument of mass communication which did, in truth, dispense knowledge "to the people from the highest to the lowest." By the 1920s, the big city daily belonged to a new collection of agencies that served the needs of the "masses" as well as the "classes," akin in this way to the department store, the street railway, or the factory. The transformation of the urban newspaper, of course, dramatically changed the role of the press in Canadian society.

I

Looking back, the sixty years between Confederation and the Depression seem the golden age of print journalism. Almost unchallenged by other media, the press had turned itself into a superlative vehicle of information and persuasion. By the turn of the century, illiteracy had been largely defeated, except amongst the new hosts of European immigrants. In 1931, the communications of the press reached, potentially, every adult Canadian: a comparison of circulation and census figures reveals there were roughly four periodicals and newspapers per household. Publishing was ranked among the leading businesses of the new industrial Canada. In 1929, newspapers and periodicals generated nearly $50 million of revenue from advertising alone. Overall, printing and publishing stood roughly mid-way in the industrial hierarchy, employing over 35,000 people to produce goods valued at $140 million in some 1,800 establishments.

The press, though, was not a brotherhood of equals. How could it be, given the diversity of country weeklies, class periodicals and national magazines, small and big city dailies? Each group served different publics. There was, above all, a chasm between the interests of the lesser media, which spoke to small or select audiences, and the ambitions of the mass media, which were engaged in the business of mass communication. The editors of the lesser journals resented the competition of their mammoth rivals. And the managers of big city dailies were often contemptuous of the problems that beset small town journalism. Publishers recognized this natural antagonism in 1919 when, after a few years of desultory feuding, they scrapped the old Canadian Press Association to launch three new organizations for country weeklies, periodicals and magazines, and daily newspapers.

Although affected by the phenomenon of mass communication, the lesser media (much like their colonial predecessors) catered to the particular needs of relatively small constituencies in ways that remained quite eccentric. Most numerous were the journals which served a locality: in 1931, some 750 country weeklies, seventy-odd town semi-weeklies and small city dailies, and an unknown number of suburban weeklies. The latter were, by and large, advertising sheets with only a smidgen of news and comment. But even legitimate local journalism, while it did provide a comfortable living for many publishers, was the weak sister of the profession. Soon after Confederation, the business and the prestige of the local press had been endangered by metropolitan invaders. In the prewar years, publishers of local newspapers disturbed the annual meetings of the Canadian Press Association with complaints about the advertising competition of city weeklies, cheap dailies, and mail-order catalogues. Even at home all was not happy because too many markets were overstocked with competitors, a problem only solved when the weakest were killed off. For instance, Belleville in 1891 had two competitors, each with a daily and a weekly, but only one daily in 1931; Barrie had four weeklies in 1891, slimmed down to two in 1931. A fair number of publishers of country weeklies tried to ease their burdens by joining a syndicate which supplied them with assorted features and advertising, commonly called "boiler plate." McKim's *Newspaper Directory* of 1911 included mention of the "Hamilton Newspaper Union List," purportedly comprehending seventy-five country weeklies with a sworn circulation of 52,000. Undeniably, the local press had lost stature in the public debate, too many newspapers merely parroting urban views, some weeklies dropping altogether editorials on national issues. Within their own communities, weeklies were often hobbled by allegiance to a local bigwig, be he a politician with a share in the newspaper or a businessman with a large advertising account. Besides, the country publisher, however enterprising, could rarely keep a good reporter since local journalism was the training-ground for the big city papers. In short, a generally mediocre local press might have been expected.

There were, nonetheless, outstanding country weeklies. A single example must suffice, that of Robert Sellar and the *Canadian Gleaner* of Huntingdon, Québec. Sellar, a Scottish immigrant who acquired his skills at the Toronto *Globe*, came to Huntingdon in 1863 at the urging of Reform notables desirous of a trustworthy organ. He would publish the *Gleaner* almost continuously for the next fifty years, until his death in 1919. Sellar proved an outspoken, eccentric champion of the Anglo-Protestant farmers in the Eastern Townships. I say eccentric because of his eclectic mixture of dogmas: an old-fashioned radicalism, of the Grit school, that idealized the yeoman farmer and the gospel of free trade; a Protestant extremism that was riddled with anti-Catholic bigotry and that idealized the separation of church and state; and a deep-seated loyalty to British connection and British ways, buoyed up by notions of Anglo-Saxon superiority. So armed, Sellar sallied forth to do battle with Catholic prelates, lying politicians, French-Canadian nationalists, and assorted big businessmen. While in the midst of such campaigns, he also gave attention to local improvement schemes, the merits of educational and agricultural reform, good roads, and temperance. In time, his vigour, and especially his passionate nativism, won him a Canada-wide notoriety. Yet his life was something of a tragedy. He witnessed the slow wasting away of the Anglo-Protestant community of the Townships as its children left for the cities or points west, their place taken by French Catholics. Sellar charged, particularly in his polemic *The Tragedy of Quebec* (1907), this cultural genocide had resulted from an ecclesiastical conspiracy to make Québec a purely Catholic enclave. Also preying on his mind was a sense of betrayal, the recognition that the Montréal business community had refused to fight for its agrarian brethren. After his death, ironically, his sons turned the *Gleaner* into a conventional weekly which, if it lost its early fame, did make money.

Sellar's story highlights the significance of the local press, more especially the country weeklies, as the voice of rural Canada. The record of local affairs these journals supplied reinforced the individuality of their towns and the surrounding farm settlements, preserving a pride of place. The better newspapers articulated the distress the leaders of the countryside felt over the spreading power of the big city and the apparent popularity of its ways. On occasion, the country weeklies and town dailies brought into the public debate a different perspective rooted in the traditional life of the countryside. In all, the local press perpetuated the reality of the Canadian mosaic.

Similar were the class journals, from dailies to monthlies, which catered to the ethnic, religious, economic, and even recreational interests of New and native-born Canadians. That strange species of sectarian warriors, born at mid-century, enjoyed its palmiest years during the 1870s and 1880s. The Montreal *Witness* continued an adamant critic of Catholic and Conservative rule in Québec, more and more distressed by the racialism of the francophone establishment that supposedly menaced the survival of English Québec. The Irish Catholic network of papers, briefly including two dailies (Montreal *Post*, 1878-1888, and Toronto *Evening Canadian*, 1882-1884), saw its demand for justice in Canada and home rule in Ireland become a leading political issue during the 1880s. That paled in comparison with the impact of the ultramontane champions of French Québec, righteous dailies like *Le Nouveau Monde* (1867-1881) and *L'Étendard* (1883-1893) or strident weeklies like *Le Franc Parleur* (1870-1878) and *La Vérité* (1881-1904).[2] Their intransigence was so extraordinary that they frightened the more moderate bishops in the church (and even the extreme Mgr. Laflèche denounced the nationalist zeal of *L'Étendard* and *La Vérité* in 1887). For the ultramontane newspapers were intent, whatever the cost, upon transforming Québec into a French enclave of the purest Catholicism, which would stand forth as the bastion of Christian civilization in a diseased North America. Time and again, these scolds disturbed the peace of church and state, in particular the Conservative party, with their clarion cries against Orangemen, freemasons, liberalism, materialism, and corruption. Beyond all else, the papers fostered amongst the well-educated a rigorously conservative perspective, at odds with the emerging industrial society, that would influence the French-Canadian establishment well into the twentieth century. Even these ideologues, however, became victims of the very modernity they so despised. During the early 1890s, the ultramontane champion virtually disappeared, much to the relief of party politicians and some churchmen. By 1900, its Irish Catholic compatriot was also extinct, though some journals lasted as diocesan organs. The daily *Witness* survived, really stagnated, until 1913, when it too passed away. What killed the sectarian press was the onslaught of mass journalism, the success of which starved the old-fashioned journal of opinion for funds.

More fortunate was the immigrant or ethnic press, by and large a post-1900 creation that grew out of the so-called fourth wave of immigration from continental Europe during the Laurier boom. In 1931, there were Ukrainian, Polish, German, and Italian weeklies as well as Jewish, Chinese, and even Japanese dailies, mostly located in Canada's big cities. These papers were often the organs of particular associations or churches, poorly financed but opinionated, sometimes factional but enjoying a fair circulation. Indeed, Watson Kirkconnell estimated roughly one newspaper for every seven "European Canadians" (some two million people) in 1931. The immigrant paper linked the newcomers into a community, informed them of affairs in the homeland, familiarized them with the ways of their new country, perhaps even raised the educational level of its readers. Overall, the ethnic newspapers were definitely an obstacle to the assimilative influences of the majority society — witness the emphasis of these papers upon the preservation of language and traditions. Yet, as often, they endeavoured to speed the adjustment of the minorities to their new condition. Such a contradictory role could lead to disaster, since (as the fate of the Irish Catholics and their journals demonstrated) adjustment might well mean absorption. Still, amongst the new Canadians, even largely assimilated elements like the Icelandic or German communities maintained their own periodicals.

The church newspapers proper were much more influential in the broader society. This press had originated at mid-century, boomed in the early twentieth century, and stabilized by the end of the 1920s. Some of these newspapers, like the *New Outlook* of the United Church, reached a nationwide audience. The Catholic church of Québec, though, boasted the most impressive group of papers. The church had set out to create anew a Christian press with the founding of *L'Action Catholique* in 1907, a Québec City daily. This flagship was soon joined by a fleet of country weeklies, such as the reorganized *Le Progrès de Chicoutimi* (1912), the new *Le Messager de Saint-Michel* (1917), and the purchased *L'Action Populaire* of Joliette (1918). On the Ontario flank, clergy and laity supported *Le Droit,* an Ottawa daily born in 1913 to voice the Franco-Ontarian plea for bilingual education in the Regulation 17 controversy. Further, in 1919 the church organized l'Union des Bulletins parossiaux, which by 1935 comprehended eighty monthlies and weeklies. Catholic and Protestant, the church press had been the great champion of those twin Christian responses to the ills of industrialism in prewar Canada, the social gospel and Catholic corporatism. By the 1920s, a natural puritanical bias made this press look askance at the hedonistic materialism of an urban Canada caught up in the flapper era. Indeed, the Protestant newspapers found themselves engaged in a fierce and losing struggle to save a dry Canada from the revitalized host of drunkards, brewers, and scheming politicians who yearned for a return to the days of easy boozing (or so it seemed). For everywhere the church press now constituted the embattled conscience of the nation, and a Victorian conscience at that, which worked to perpetuate the social and moral verities — from the sanctity of marriage to the necessity of a Christian sabbath — of the nineteenth century.

Both the ethnic and church newspapers, however, were outnumbered by the spokesmen of Canada's material pursuits. A huge variety of specialized organs had arisen since the late nineteenth century to serve almost every producer. Oldest was a flourishing agrarian press for wheat-growers, dairymen, cattle-breeders, even beekeepers that acted as the vehicle for the causes of scientific and business agriculture, thereby to convert farmers into up-to-date producers able to function effectively in the marketplace. Nearly as old, the papers for lawyers, engineers, doctors, and dentists were staid proponents of professional excellence, with the occasional crusader like Wallace Seccombe's *Oral Health*. These had been joined by associational publications for bankers, insurance men, and manufacturers — such as that lusty advocate of the growth ethic, *Industrial Canada*, fittingly launched by the Canadian Manufacturers' Association with the new century in 1900. Much less prominent, though very profitable and lively, were the trades' papers of John Bayne Maclean: *Canadian Grocer* (1887), *Hardware and Metal* (1888), *Dry Goods Review* (1891) and on and on with such exotic titles as *Men's Wear*, *Canadian Machinery*, and even *Power House*. On the other side of the class line was the trade union organ — one of the first apparently the *Trades Journal* (1880) of Springhill, Nova Scotia, for the Provincial Workmen's Association. Such papers furnished an assortment of news and views, sometimes strident depending upon the bias of the union. Witness the *Canadian Trade Unionist* (1921), initially the champion of the Canadian Federation of Labour in its left-wing and nationalist campaign against the international unions.

Set apart by its apparent breadth of view was the specialized journal of opinion, which purported to speak for the farmer, business, or labour. Foremost again, the agrarian advocates won the greatest audience. Most famous were the *Farmers' Sun* of the 1890s in Ontario and the *Grain Growers' Guide* of the new century on the prairies, both prominent and even feared voices of that sporadic farm revolt inspired by early industrialism. By the mid-1920s the *Guide* had been joined by *Le Bulletin de La Ferme* and the *Western Producer*, all of which pushed the virtues of cooperation upon the farmer — the most valuable technique of improvement born by that revolt. In particular, Saskatchewan's *Western Producer* proved a vital publicist of the Wheat Pool movement in its rapid spread across the prairies. Equally vigorous were their enemies, the financial papers like the long-standing *Monetary Times* (Toronto, 1867) or the *Journal of Commerce* (Montréal 1875) and the newer *Financial Post* (Toronto, 1907) or *Financial Times* (Montréal, 1912) which gave coverage to the whole business scene. If most useful to their readers for their business news, these papers were also the leading spokesmen of free enterprise in the Canadian media. During the 1920s, for instance, Maclean's *Financial Post* waged a wordy war against big government and the Bolshevik menace that threatened to halt the onward rush of Canadian prosperity. It is only fair to add, though, that the *Post* also lambasted the CMA and big business in general for its shady ethics and assorted stupidities. At the bottom of the heap, again, lay the socialist weeklies which, however vigorous, were poor and often ephemeral. Few remained independent for very long, even a popular eccentric like *Cotton's Weekly* (Cowansville, 1911) finding it expedient to join forces with a labour body or socialist sect. And yet, they too were important: these weeklies shaped the traditions of the working class in early industrial Canada and criticized, vociferously, the capitalist system which in so many ways seemed unjust to the labouring man. Together, the specialized journals mobilized what were distinct social and economic interests in a struggle for national pre-eminence, and so added a new dimension to the already complex expression of the Canadian mosaic.

Off in their own little domain were the true journals of opinion, a colourful crew of happy debaters that seemed to relish discussion, if not controversy, for its own sake. Their numbers included a series of highbrow reviews, somewhat aloof from the hurly-burly of life: the *Revue Canadienne* (1864-1922) which dealt with the culture of man as well as public affairs from a conservative and Catholic standpoint; the *Canadian Monthly* (1872-1882) and later the Toronto *Week* (1883-1896) which attempted to inject a moral and philosophical element into the national debate; the academic rivals, the usually liberal *Queen's Quarterly* (1893) and the always conservative *University Magazine* (1907-1920) which debated the merits of Laurier's Canada; or the excellent *Canadian Forum* (1920), during the 1920s trying vainly to broaden the political and artistic horizons of the country. Much more pugnacious (and ephemeral) were a wider assortment of crusading journals intent upon speeding to victory some cause or other, be it social reform or a particular nationalism. The temperance and moral reform legions in English Canada sponsored a host of such papers over the years. But what were called "les journals de combat" were especially prominent in French Québec: amongst the best known was Olivar Asselin's *Le Nationaliste* (1904-1910), a spokesman for the new century's liberal nationalism. In fact, many such papers flared briefly but brightly, causing the occasional politician or churchman upset. No doubt, the journal of opinion did act as a source of new concerns or new ideas which sometimes percolated down to the public. Usually its influence was slight though, in large part because the audience was so small and impotent. That was true even in French Québec where the nationalist weeklies and monthlies never amounted to more than a very minor power in the land. Abbé Groulx's frenetic *L'Action Française* of the 1920s, for example, may have reflected the anxieties of some intellectuals, but it had little impact upon public policy or debate. The import of the journal of opinion remained its contribution to the depth and variety of intellectual life in the country. Otherwise, it was the most insignificant of the lesser media.

One journal of opinion, though, needs to be singled out for special distinction — Bob Edwards' humourous Calgary *Eye Opener* (1902-1922). Now humour and satire were not unknown to Canadian journalism. During the late nineteenth century, J. W. Bengough's cartoons in *Grip* savaged the mighty men of politics and society for a sophisticated clientele. But the *Eye Opener* was different. For this "Great Moral Weekly" was the satirical voice of an unregenerate lowbrow. Bob Edwards was a Scottish-born adventurer who, after assorted travels, settled down to a life of intermittent alcoholism and journalism in Alberta.

His eight-page weekly appeared irregularly, depending upon his sobriety, sold for five cents on the streets, and eventually on the trains of the Canadian Pacific Railway. By 1911, the *Eye Opener* enjoyed a circulation of some 26,000 copies in Calgary and throughout the prairies, its fame reaching into Great Britain as well as the United States. What so charmed readers was the *Eye Opener*'s compilation of news, gossip, scandal, speculation, fantasy, wit, homilies, and fun — all enthused with a love of the ordinary person. Edwards used his weekly to survey the low life of the horse races, prize fights, drinking spots, and the like; to ridicule the pretentions of high society, the "holier-than-thou" attitudes of the moralists, the greed of big business, the stupidity and corruption of politicians; to champion reforms like old-age pensions, women's rights, minimum wage laws, even briefly prohibition. Perhaps he was most famous for his imaginary characters, the British remittance man, Albert Buzzard-Cholomondeley, and the small town editor, Peter J. McGonigle of the "Midnapore Gazette," whose comments poked fun at western ways. The *Eye Opener* had no particular impact, even if its satire irritated the high and mighty (once, Lord Strathcona of CPR fame who almost sued for libel). The point is the weekly's very existence spoke well of a Canada already too notorious for its straight-laced morality and pomposity.

Of quite a different magnitude was the magazine press. That press typically constitutes a national medium reaching out to all citizens to convey common ideas, a national awareness, even a sense of identity. In countries like the United States or Canada, without national dailies comparable to England's London newspapers, the importance of vigorous magazines to nation-building is obvious. The United States was fortunate, boasting at an early date a healthy variety of magazines. The nineteenth-century literary reviews, such as *Scribner's* or *Harper's*, had won, by and large, only a bourgeois audience, though both in the city and the countryside. Their prosperity had depended, primarily, upon subscription revenues. Toward the end of the century, Cyrus Curtis, Frank Munsey, and other entrepreneurs launched new popular magazines, low in price, full of advertising, and aimed at a mass market. Their publications offered a wide range of matter, from happy biographies of the famous to a great deal of light fiction, which promised to entertain, and so please, as many readers as possible. For the mass magazine made its profits out of the wealth of advertising attracted by a huge circulation. Once, what little advertising there was had been restricted to the front and back pages; but soon, symbolic of their new import, ads were spread throughout almost all the pages of the magazine, sometimes overwhelming the other contents. No matter, the mass magazines before long were setting new records for gross circulation and profit.

Canada was not so fortunate. Its magazine press only emerged from the ranks of the lesser media after the Great War, and even by 1931 that press remained a peculiarly truncated, and very uneasy, mass medium. The source of its ills lay in the commercial situation facing the publisher. The key to his success was to find a special, preferably nationwide public — snobs or plebeians, housewives or sportsmen — which had not previously been exploited by others. That posed an initial difficulty in a country so large and diverse as Canada, with a small scattered population divided into two main language groups. The great obstacle, however, was the early penetration of the Canadian market by American magazines. Throughout the nineteenth century, American periodicals had circulated freely in Canada. Naturally, when the mass magazine was born in the United States at the end of the century, its pioneers looked upon Canada as merely another, hitherto unexploited, market for their wares. Readers responded eagerly: neither British imports nor native productions could compare in price or appeal. As early as 1911, McKim's *Directory* listed a Canadian edition of *Collier's*, published in Toronto, with a circulation of 60,000. After the war, this penetration become an overwhelming invasion — in 1931 the total value of American newspapers and magazines imported into Canada was well over $4 million. The most popular were the middlebrow and "trashy" imports: Sunday newspapers, love and romance pulps, the family weeklies like *Liberty* or *Saturday Evening Post, McCall's* for women and *True Story* for men. Apparently, the invasion had less success in Québec where language was a barrier, but swept Nova Scotia and especially the west. In any case, the circulation of American imports far surpassed the circulation of native magazines in the Dominion as a whole. Little wonder magazine publishers, in league with nationalists and puritans, mounted a campaign during the twenties for a cultural tariff to block the entry of this "alien" propaganda.

The Canadian magazines that had withstood such stiff competition were of two sorts, the old-fashioned survivors of the late nineteenth century and a flashy crew of Americanized newcomers. Numbered in the first camp were long-standing literary periodicals like *Le Samedi* (36,258),[3] religious magazines such as *La Voix Nationale* (37,877), and Christian family weeklies like the *Northern Messenger* (69,328). More prominent was *Saturday Night* (30,507), begun in 1887 as a society paper for Toronto but converted during the prewar years into an opinionated review of life with a definite snob appeal. Its message during the 1920s was a mixture of optimism and conservatism, spiced with a certain anxiety over the Bolshevik threat. Most successful, though, were the rural magazines, in particular the *Prairie Farmer* (149,572), the weekly edition of the Winnipeg *Free Press*, and the *Family Herald* (217,247), the property of the Montreal *Star*. The *Family Herald*, subtitled "Canada's National Farm Journal," was an impressive compilation of short reports on farm affairs, a news summary, and assorted delights for a family audience. At first much like other urban weeklies designed for the farmer, aggressive promotion had shot its circulation ahead of all rivals in the late 1880s and early 1890s: suffi-cient to inspire complaints from western journalists about unfair "foreign" competition. After 1900, its editors built upon that success by slowly diversifying and popularizing its contents to produce a weekly, illustrated magazine with a personality distinct from the daily. The outlook of the *Family Herald*, however, remained steadfastly Victorian and British, even beyond 1930.

The newer, popular magazines imitated, often slavishly, the Ameri-can lead. Ironically, the most successful were again the children of newspapers, weekend magazines such as the Saturday *La Presse* (170,029), the Montreal *Standard* (120,391), the *Star Weekly* (211,607), and the *Sunday Province* of Vancouver (91,450). According to J. H. Cranston, the editor in the 1910s and 1920s, the *Star Weekly* was clear-ing upwards of half a million dollars a year prior to the Depression. The weekly began in 1910 as a very proper review of public affairs and the cultural scene. It flopped. Just prior to the war, Cranston started to emulate the formula of the American Sunday newspapers, filling the weekly's pages with a variety of snappy news items, short entertaining stories, fiction and comics, plenty of illustrations — much of this from American suppliers. By and large, though, these happy weekend magazines — the *Star Weekly*, for instance, was a great champion of naive optimism — avoided the vulgarity and sensationalism associated with their American mentors.

Less prosperous was a small group of independent, "true" maga-zines: the two household monthlies, the *Canadian Home Journal* (131,885) and the *National Home Monthly* (103,412);[4] the *Canadian Magazine* (89,729), an old literary review recently spruced up to win a wider family audience; and two semi-popular literary magazines, *La Revue Populaire* (26,547) and *La Revue Moderne* (21,107). Founded in 1919, *La Revue Moderne* was initially a hightoned, staid, and Catholic women's monthly with the proud mission of advancing Québec's na-tive culture. That soon changed. The magazine dropped its pretentions to high culture so as to win the French-Canadian housewife with illust-rations and photographs, colour advertising, much fiction, and wom-en's service items. At the bottom of the list stood a variety of spe-cialized magazines devoted to geography, pulp fiction, and recre-ational pursuits like yachting, motoring, movies, fishing, or golf. None apparently did well, partly because of the competition of newspaper offerings, but even more because of the popularity of similar American types.

Canada did boast one chain of magazines, the hearty creations of that publishing genius, John Bayne Maclean. This son of a Methodist minis-ter, endowed with a capacity for hard work and a fertile imagination, had made his fortune through trade and business periodicals. But he was ambitious to imitate the fame of American publishers of mass magazines, notably of his bosom-buddy the notorious Frank Munsey.

Maclean's first venture was *Maclean's Magazine* (1905), originally a general interest digest for businessmen which specialized in reprints, full or condensed, from the world's periodicals. Just prior to the war, Maclean and his editor, T. B. Costain, began to alter the character of the magazine so that it might cover the Canadian scene. By the mid-1920's, *Maclean's* sported the set of offerings that would remain roughly standard for forty odd years — articles on Canadian people or things Canadian, some native fiction, regular departments for women and men, all complete with illustrations, some photographs, a bit of colour, and much advertising. Maclean then added *Canadian Homes and Gardens* (1925) and *Mayfair* (1927) for the upper crust (Maclean, himself, was an inveterate social climber who loved the doings of high society) and *Chatelaine* (1928) for the ordinary, married woman. All the Maclean enterprises were modelled upon the format and formulas developed by similar American types; all were emphatically Canadian, using Canadian authors, concentrating on Canadian life, and boosting Canadian ways. The combination worked. *Maclean's* and its compatriots were welcomed into many a comfortable and proper household across English Canada.[5]

II

At the top of the press hierarchy, of course, were the big city dailies. The transformation of the colonial daily into the modern mass newspaper was closely tied to the emergence of industrial Canada. The reading public increased enormously because of the general advance of literacy, the growth of the city population, and above all its apparently unquenchable thirst for news and entertainment. Indeed, the escalating demand for newspapers far outpaced the increase in the numbers of new, literate urbanites. Publishers were able to respond because the new print technology, a plentiful supply of inexpensive newsprint, and a flood of advertising allowed them to mass produce a relatively cheap product. Supply and demand were intimately linked, the very growth of newspaper circulations fostering greater public interest in reading and business interest in advertising. Newspapers were always the best promoters of the patronage of the press. So, by 1931, there was roughly one daily published for every household in Canada, though in fact two-thirds of the actual circulation of the daily press occurred in metropolitan areas where many families purchased more than one newspaper a day.

The mass daily had not sprung full-blown upon the Canadian scene. Rather the transformation was a long, drawn-out process originating in the 1870s, characterized by a general mutation of newspapers which began during the 1890s, and reaching completion only in the 1920s. The background to this transformation was a rapid expansion of the daily press during the late nineteenth and early twentieth centuries. There was a near doubling of numbers in a mere seventeen years, from forty-six dailies in 1874 to ninety-one in 1891. That growth continued during the years of the Laurier boom until 1913, when the country had 138 daily newspapers. Much of the expansion was accounted for by the appearance of dailies in western Canada, but by no means all — there were some journalists who found money sufficient to launch newcomers in the cities of the older provinces.

Initially responsible, as before Confederation, were politicians and their minions who strove to construct countrywide networks of outright organs. During the 1870s, Conservative notables began such "new-style" champions, more newsworthy and more loyal, as the Toronto *Mail* (1872), the Halifax *Herald* (1875), the St. John *Sun* (1878), and the Winnipeg *Times* (1879). Likewise, in Québec, the Liberal party sponsored *La Patrie* (1879) in Montréal and *L'Électeur* (1880) in Québec City, finally giving the francophone wing of the party a forceful voice in press debate. Ambitious politicos added to the lists of partisan journals in the 1880s: F.-X. Trudel's ultramontane standard-bearer, *L'Étendard* (1883) of Montréal; N. F. Davin's Conservative paper, the Regina *Leader* (1883); or Carter-Cotton's *News-Advertiser* (1886) of Vancouver, also Conservative. Indeed, the 1880s probably marked the high point of party journalism in Canada.

But the outstanding event was the renaissance of the popular press. A few perceptive entrepreneurs, mostly in central Canada, founded self-declared "people's journals" modelled, so it would seem, upon the practices of New York journalists like James Gordon Bennett, Jr. and Joseph Pulitzer. The eventual leaders in the ranks of this, the Canadian version of the New Journalism then sweeping western Europe and the United States, were the *Star* (1869) and *La Presse* (1884) of Montréal; the *Telegram* (1876), the *World* (1880), the *News* (1881), and the *Star* (1892) of Toronto; the Ottawa *Journal* (1885); and the Hamilton *Herald* (1889). By and large, the people's journals were one-cent evening dailies which combined sensational practices, maverick politics, and much local news to win the support of the less sophisticated and less prosperous readers in Canada's cities. Democrats by instinct, these dailies displayed a contempt for social convention and a disrespect for established authority linked to a faith in the wisdom of the common man and a deep admiration for success. The renaissance of the popular press destroyed the unity of form and style and appeal that had characterized the dailies of a generation earlier. Suddenly newspapers differed: at one extreme was the traditional, elitist organ like the Montreal *Gazette* or *La Minerve*, and at the other extreme was the innovative, populist paper like the Montreal *Star* or *La Presse*. Canada, briefly, seemed on the way to a daily press divided along class lines, as in Europe.

Nearly all publishers, however, came to emphasize the quantity of readers over the quality of readers. They strove to increase circulation in order to generate more advertising revenue which would cover rising expenses and ensure a healthy profit. That set off a vicious cycle of circulation wars: publishers cut the prices of their newspapers, spruced up their contents, launched multiple editions, embarked on stunts or crusades, and gave away innumerable gifts. Some newspapers earned huge sums of money, Hugh Graham of the Montreal *Star* and John Ross Robertson of the Toronto *Telegram* eventually becoming self-made millionaires. More newspapers, their publishers unable or unwilling to engage in the brutal warfare, fell by the wayside. Most dramatic was the decimation of the francophone press, to be specific the death of the old-fashioned journal of opinion which had attained its purest expression in Québec. Over a twelve-year period, seven dailies, some of considerable antiquity, ceased publication: *Le Journal de Québec* in 1889, *La Justice* in 1892, *Le Canadien* in 1893, *L'Étendard* in 1893, *La Minerve* in 1899, *Le Monde Canadien* in 1900, and *Le Courrier du Canada* in 1901. In general, though, the circulation wars had inspired the popularization of the daily press. Established party newspapers stooped to conquer a mass audience by emulating the innovations of the people's journals. At the end of 1890s, for example, *La Patrie* and *L'Événement* escaped death by imitating the immensely successful *La Presse*.

Even so, the daily press of Laurier's Canada catered to an assortment of publics. Take the example of Montréal in 1910. In the anglophone camp were the *Gazette*, a highbrow morning newspaper that championed a business-minded convervatism and reached an audience well beyond the city's confines; the *Star*, a one-cent evening paper, boisterous and popular, a Conservative maverick that managed to combine a vague radicalism with a fierce imperialism; the *Witness*, now old-fashioned and still discernably Christian; and a tired *Herald*, Liberal but otherwise nondescript. In the francophone camp were *La Presse*, vulgar and sensationalist, radical but Liberal, which boasted the largest daily circulation in Canada; *La Patrie*, also popular if less outlandish, a maverick Conservative; the morning *Le Canada*, a new high-toned Liberal organ; and *Le Devoir*, just founded, a nationalist daily for the sophisticated and cultured reader. Indeed, the daily press of French Québec was still split into two sometimes hostile groups: the elite journals of opinion (*L'Action Catholique, Le Canada,* and *Le Devoir*) which spoke to the intellect of the province and the popular journals of news (*Le Soleil, L'Événement, La Patrie,* and *La Presse*) which reached the urban masses.

The competition among newspapers, at bottom, rested upon a peculiar balance of economic and social forces. Although running a newspaper was an expensive task, it was possible for newcomers to start and maintain a big city daily in a cluttered market. Paper prices and wages were low, political money was still available, advertising revenues were growing, and the public was reading more. This situation allowed J. S. Willison's Toronto *News* to survive against five other more prosperous rivals. Willison was one of the most admired journalists of his generation. He won his fame during the 1890s as the editor of the Toronto *Globe*, a newspaper which he rescued from the doldrums it suffered in the years following George Brown's death. Success spoiled Willison for party journalism, though, and he began to yearn for a chance to run an independent newspaper that could speak out freely on all public issues. Fortunately, he found a wealthy patron, J. W. Flavelle, whose sense of public duty inspired him to finance Willison's dream. In 1902, the two men teamed up to buy the *News*, then a decrepit evening newspaper, for $150,000. Willison's *News* proved a strange but not unpleasing blend of popular offerings and an old-style editorial page. It was never a commercial success, perhaps because it was so preachy. The paper's financial statement for 1907 showed total earnings of almost $200,000 of which fully $142,000 came from advertising. Its operating expenses were $232,000, paper costs making up a mere $63,000. The loss was transferred to what was euphemistically called the "betterment account," which now stood at $255,000.[6] So unprofitable a newspaper, it might be thought, was doomed. By no means. In 1908, Flavelle managed to negotiate a sale to a syndicate of Conservatives headed by Frank Cochrane, a provincial minister and party bagman, which finalized the return of the *News* and Willison to the ranks of party journalism. The point is that even unsound enterprises, and there were others like the *News*, could survive in a time of heady optimism and easy money engendered by the Laurier boom.

The crunch was bound to come. The time of troubles began with the sharp recession of 1913, worsened due to wartime inflation, and continued almost unabated into the early 1920s because of postwar instability. Advertising revenues lagged. Wages rose. The price of newsprint, in particular, skyrocketed — from just under $2.00 per 100 lb delivered in 1908 to $5.67 per 100 lb for carload lots f.o.b. Canadian mills in 1921. Doubtful enterprises disappeared, either outright or more often in mergers. Between 1914 and 1922, forty dailies ceased publication, almost all in the overstocked anglophone camp. Many of these deaths occurred in small cities, but included in the total were such papers as the *News* (now called the *Times*) and the *World* of Toronto, the Winnipeg *Telegram*, and the Vancouver *News-Advertiser*. This slimming of press ranks slowed down with the return of prosperity after 1921. In fact, further disappearances were balanced by new arrivals, which left Canada with just over one hundred dailies in 1931.

The time of troubles had a marked impact upon the practices of daily journalism. Business principles were now, by necessity, uppermost in the minds of owners. The typical daily newspaper in postwar Canada was treated, first and foremost, as an ordinary commercial property required to earn its keep and turn a profit. Some papers, like the monopolistic dailies, had little difficulty succeeding. By 1931, there were forty single-daily centres, admittedly almost all towns and small cities. Happier were the big cities where the time of troubles had not eliminated all rival papers: St. John and Winnipeg had two dailies, Ottawa and Vancouver three, Québec City and Toronto four, and Montréal an astonishing eight. Yet the era of cutthroat competition was over. Wisely, at least from a business standpoint, publishers came to a series of tacit agreements to divvy up the profits available. In 1926, General V. W. Oldham moved the Vancouver *Star* out of the evening field while R. J. Cromie of the rival *Sun* left the morning market, each acquiring the readers thereby deserted. By 1919, the *Citizen* and the *Journal* of Ottawa had entered upon a formal partnership, complete for a time with a transfer of stocks, to sponsor joint circulation campaigns and share surplus advertising revenues. Going a step further, Hugh Graham actually purchased the rival *Herald* and the Southams the Hamilton *Times*, newspapers they continued to publish to prevent any new outbreak of competition. This ploy pointed to another sign of the times, the emergence of the newspaper chain. The chief gobbler of newspaper properties was the incredible Southam family. Their initial fortunes based upon the Hamilton *Spectator* and a printing company, the Southams had acquired the Ottawa *Citizen* in 1897, the Calgary *Herald* in 1908, the Edmonton *Journal* in 1912, the Winnipeg *Tribune* in 1920, and the Vancouver *Province* in 1923. A smaller and more recent chain was the Sifton holdings, which by the end of the 1920s included the Winnipeg *Free Press*, the Regina *Leader-Post*, and the Saskatoon *Star-Phoenix*. What capped this march toward oligopoly was the completion of the "Canadian Press" in the mid-1920s. "CP" was a news cooperative, owned by the publishers, which could and did deny franchise rights to prospective newcomers on the grounds their competition would threaten the profits of existing newspapers. That made it very difficult for any entrepreneur to break into a city already served by a daily newspaper. The rationalization of the press scene during the 1920s signalled the close of the heyday of entrepreneurialism. The newspaper industry was a business like any other, wherein reigned the twin gods of Profit and Stability.

No less striking was the change in the daily newspaper itself. "The aim of the ordinary newspaper is to be all things to all men," wrote W. D. Lesueur as early as 1903.[7] True enough, there remained a distinction, in tone at least, between morning and evening newspapers. The morning dailies, roughly one-quarter of the total, like the Toronto *Globe* or the Montreal *Gazette* or *Le Canada* were a touch more reserved, even highbrow, aimed usually at a metropolitan audience of middle and upper income Canadians; whereas the afternoon and evening dailies like *La Presse* or the Toronto *Telegram* were flamboyant, popular sheets which appealed in particular to a local audience of middle and lower income readers. As well, each newspaper proudly claimed its own traditions and personality. The Halifax *Herald* was always a more middlebrow, more colourful newspaper than its morning rival, the *Chronicle*. By contrast, the Halifax *Star* (the *Chronicle*'s evening offshoot) was well-nigh a lowbrow daily which indulged in more sensationalism than the *Mail* (the *Herald*'s evening offshoot). Lastly, the offerings of each big city newspaper necessarily had a particular flavour suitable to the tastes of its locality. That was true even of the chain newspapers. The Southam dailies, unlike the Hearst papers in the United States, were never produced according to some rigid formula, but rather according to the individual publishers' conceptions of what their clientele desired.

These distinctions and idiosyncrasies, however, pale in comparison with the overall consistency of the daily press. Indeed, during the 1920s, hitherto unusual newspapers shed those attributes which had set them apart from the common herd. So while *La Presse* was "greyed," losing its yellow tinge and its penchant for outrageous news, *L'Action Catholique* was "coloured," losing its austere traditionalism and its disdain for modern practices. The daily newspaper was fast becoming a standardized product like the other consumer goodies produced by the industrial machine. All too often, if the packaging was different, the contents were not. The typical newspaper (what Carlton McNaught called "the department store of literature"[8]) endeavoured to reach a mass audience by supplying, if in different quantities and with a different flair, much the same kinds of information, entertainment, features, and comment. The logic of mass communication had fostered a roughly homogeneous journalism. The age of everybody's newspaper had dawned.

III

The colonial reader of yesteryear would hardly have recognized the new dailies. Perhaps most pronounced was the change in the size, format, and appearance of the newspaper. The first key shift, occurring in the 1880s and 1890s, was from the four-page paper, sometimes with nine columns of print on a large sheet, to an eight-or twelve-page paper, with six columns of print on a smaller sheet. At the same time, publishers began to produce enlarged Saturday editions filled with family features, a kind of weekly magazine that would grow ever larger in succeeding decades. In the 1890s, and pioneered by *La Presse*, most dailies cleared their front page of ads and other clutter to present important news stories. By the end of the decade, *La Presse* and the Montreal *Star* (emulating the yellow press of New York) commonly used black, flaring headlines, occasionally with a cartoon or illustration, to signal to the reader the great event of the day. After 1900, nearly all newspapers broke away from the column straitjacket, replacing the once normal array of print with headlines, photographs, boxed or double-column stories. The conventional wisdom now presumed an attractive, even brash, front page would boost newsstand sales. As the size of the daily ballooned to twenty and more pages in the 1910s and thereafter, publishers increasingly attempted to brighten and reorganize the inside pages. The more popular dailies, like the Toronto *Star*, went to great pains to carry photographs throughout; although a few morning papers, like the Montreal *Gazette*, always regarded such a practice needlessly garish. But all newspapers, morning and evening, came to devote separate departments to sports, finance, classified ads, and so on, often indexed on the front page. Things would change slightly in later decades, but by the 1920s the daily newspaper had taken on an essentially modern appearance.

The attention that the publisher lavished on his front page signified a major shift in the priorities of daily journalism. The mass newspaper excelled as a record of the present. News, not comment, was its forte. The new credo of the publisher was a promise to supply a complete coverage of life and affairs to suit everyone's, or almost everyone's taste. Note, for instance, the commitment of *Le Journal* (16 December, 1899), a Montréal daily that flourished briefly around the turn of the century: to "SATISFAIRE LA LEGITIME CURIOSITE DU PUBLIC CANADIENS-FRANCAIS." The consequence was that the reporter with his notebook became a familiar figure throughout the land, in high society and in the slums. The big city publisher employed teams of this new breed of journalist to fill the swelling pages of his daily with topical copy. The reporter and his work were clothed in legend: perhaps he was a bohemian soul, cynical if not dissipated, and always underpaid, but above all he was the impartial and ubiquitous servant of knowledge. There was some truth behind this legend. Frederick Griffin, a reporter with the Toronto *Star* in the 1920s and 1930s, was a highly skilled witness of life. He brought to his work intelligence, wit, dedication, persistence, and adaptability. He remained a generalist, able to use his talents on any story from high finance to low farce. And he was a superb wordsmith, who could translate an event into a clear, striking story that captured the reader's attention. Men and women like Griffin were indeed the eyes of the public.

The related phenomenon was the emergence of the "Canadian Press," itself a mass medium because of its importance as a disseminator of news. "CP" resulted from business necessity. The turn-of-the-century daily depended upon the cheap news of the telegraph companies, especially Canadian Pacific Telegraphs which furnished its clients with the "Associated Press" world and American reports plus a Canadian news summary. That system broke down after 1907 when a revolt by Winnipeg dailies against a rate increase ultimately led the company to withdraw from the news business. In response, publishers across the country organized the "Canadian Press," essentially a holding corporation for the Canadian rights to the "AP" copy. Immediately, the loose cooperative was wracked by the tensions endemic in an era of competitive journalism. The small city and western newspapers wanted "CP" to become a true news agency which would furnish not just the "AP" copy but panCanadian, British, even European information, thus making their task of news coverage much easier. The Montréal and Toronto dailies (some with their own news service,[9] contracts with other American agencies or newspapers, and large staffs of reporters) thought such a "CP" could not help their own news coverage (however it benefited small city competitors) and certainly would cost much money. The dispute centred on the way in which members would share the enormous costs of leased telegraph wires for a national service. If geography ruled, the cost, estimated at a third of a million dollars annually, would fall hardest upon the poorer dailies outside central Canada. In 1917, after an appeal from western publishers, Robert Borden (the Prime Minister) decided the national interest would justify a $50,000 annual subsidy to allow the inauguration of a national service. That infuriated the managers of the *Star* and *Telegram* of Toronto, who once threatened to smash the cooperative if the subsidy was increased to enable better coverage of the British scene. After 1923, the politicians themselves, much exercised by the "CP" monopoly of news, ended the subsidy. The bone of contention gone, the publishers closed ranks behind the cooperative which had quickly proved its news and business value. The Canadian daily, especially its front page, became a vehicle for the uniform messages disseminated by "CP" and "AP", sometimes supplemented or altered by copy from other agencies, foreign newspapers, or special correspondents.

The news could cover the commonplace or the unusual, the expected or the unpredictable, anything that might inform and entertain a reader. Even so, much of the news focussed either upon the public scene or the game of life. The coverage of politics and the world had always been a newspaper speciality, and so it remained. The people's journals emphasized another dimension by concentrating on the civic arena, an innovation which exploited the parochialism of the urban masses. In its first years, for instance, the Hamilton *Herald* made a big splash by reporting on the city council, the state of hospital and charity services, and the condition of local industry. All in all, morning dailies remained keenly aware of the provincial, the Ottawa, and the international spheres; whereas afternoon and evening dailies were more attentive to happenings in the local community. Every paper, of course, recorded spectacular events or important doings anywhere on the public scene.

What balanced this traditional staple was the zealous coverage more and more newspapers gave to the game of life. Really, the first eminently successful supplier of this variety of news was Trefflé Berthiaume, publisher of La Presse from the early 1890s: he devoted much of the paper's front page and almost all of its last page to news about fires, accidents, murders, scandals, distress — indeed anything that might satisfy the morbid curiosity of the masses. In fact, La Presse's innovation marked the beginning of a sixty-year "silly season" in news reports, when the most banal melodrama and pointless shenanigans would find a place in some paper somewhere. Virtually every newspaper, including the most highbrow, succumbed. But in the end none, not even La Presse, could match the zeal and the skill of the Toronto Star. During the 1920s, the Star raised what was called "razzle-dazzle journalism" to new heights, lavishing huge amounts of space upon exciting or unusual events, no matter how trivial. The function of this kind of news, obviously, was more to entertain than inform the bemused reader.

Just as important was the way the news was presented. One technique was to lard the paper with assorted tidbits of news. A front page with upwards of twenty-five items from hither and thither was not abnormal. More common, of course, was a front page like that of the Vancouver Province of 1 May, 1925. Thereon were sixteen items, the longest detailing the capture of a Wong Foon Sing supposedly involved in a juicy affair called the "Janet Smith murder." Amongst the rest were reports on Ottawa doings, the Prince of Wales in Capetown, a suspicious train wreck in the German-Polish corridor, three ships in distress off Halifax, and an Englishwoman's troubles in entering a church where a jazz band was playing to the congregation. The other technique was to provide a massive coverage of a big story, complete with photographs, interviews, and long reports on the front and inside pages. While most papers might sometimes employ this approach, the Toronto Star excelled at it. Soon after acquiring the Star in 1899, Joe Atkinson established the practice of turning loose his entire army of reporters to cover a big story, and clearing the news columns of all ordinary matter to carry everything pertinent to that story. McKinley's assassination in 1901, the Gamey bribery scandal of 1903, the Toronto fire of 1904, and the San Francisco earthquake of 1906 were some of the first topics so treated. Once the immediate news interest had been exhausted, of course, Atkinson dropped the massive coverage and the Star returned to normal. If abbreviated news and massive coverage were opposite extremes, both created that necessary illusion of knowledge upon which now rested much of the popular appeal of the daily.

Obviously, the news of the mass daily was tinted a mild shade of yellow. "What is a newspaper published for if not to produce a sensation," the Hamilton Herald (6 May, 1890) asked, "to make an impression upon its readers and the public?" That axiom spread from the people's journals to the whole of the daily press. Sometime around the turn of the century, the search for scoops became an all-consuming passion with news editors. Reporters vied with each other, indeed fought with each other, to get the first report of an event and, preferably, the exclusive rights to the story. Frederick Griffin was an especially adept scoopster, ready to lie, cheat, fly, and even snowshoe to get the news. Equally common was the "human interest" story with its emphasis upon people, their hopes and fears and habits, with which an ordinary reader could easily identify. At its best this technique lent itself to a trenchant analysis of life — such as the reports of the *News* in the 1880s and the *Star* in the 1900s upon the plight of Toronto's poor; at its worst the human interest story was merely anecdotal and sentimental — such as the tedious portraits of happy Catholic families that occasionally appeared on the inside pages of Berthiaume's *La Presse*. A third practice was the newspaper stunt, an example of news created to excite the public. In April of 1888, the Montreal *Star* organized a pick and shovel brigade to dramatize the need to clean up the winter filth that clogged Montréal's streets; in March of 1901, *La Presse* financed the voyage of a ship from Montréal to the Atlantic to demonstrate the year-round navigability of the St. Lawrence; and in January of 1923, the Toronto *Star* boomed the story of a supposed wild boy, the Jacques Richtor case, later exploiting the news that its own investigations had disclosed he was a fake. Closely related to the stunt were the crusades, exposés and interviews (and editorials, of course) designed to sway public opinion. Over the years, the Toronto *Telegram* waged innumerable campaigns on behalf of the little man against all kinds of civic extravagance; just as the Montreal *Star* fought against Canadian or rather Liberal cowardice on behalf of a united Empire. More prosaic but very common were the crusades for local improvement: the Halifax *Herald's* battle to industrialize its port city or the Lethbridge *Herald's* plea for the irrigation of the surrounding countryside, to name but two. Even an elite newspaper like *Le Devoir* might embark upon a crusade: witness its wartime assaults on Anglo-Saxon "prussianism" in the struggle to protect bilingual education in Ontario. Sensationalism was rife in the daily press because it succeeded — it won attention.

Yet strange as it may seem, by the 1920s the ideal of objectivity had fixed itself in the minds of journalists and readers as the guiding principle of proper reporting. News columns were more impartial than in times past. Reporters were trained to witness rather than interpret events, to provide copy free of any personal views. News agencies supplied factual, often bland, reports so as not to upset the editorial proclivities of client newspapers. The most obvious change was in the reporting of politics: no longer was such news normally cast in a partisan mould. During the federal election campaign of 1930, for example, the leading Halifax dailies, the Liberal *Chronicle* and the Conservative *Herald*, carried straight "CP" reports on the tours of Mackenzie King and R. B. Bennett across the country. Even so, the news columns of the mass daily were invariably biased in some fashion or other. Headlines were, in fact, editorial statements which interpreted an event, and thereby affected the reader's perception of the news. *L'Action Catholique* in 1920 understandably charged that the whole practice was false and misleading, though this paper, too, soon succumbed. News agency reports often reflected the prevailing views of their home nations. Time and again, Canadian journalists lamented the Americanized version of world and British affairs "AP," "Hearst," and eventually "UP" supplied their newspapers. More important was the effect a publisher's opinions, or a newspaper's traditions, had upon the selection and presentation of the news. During the provincial election campaign of November 1920, the Vancouver *Sun*, a Liberal newspaper, gave fulsome coverage to the Liberal premier (Honest John Oliver) and his cronies while largely neglecting his Conservative opponent (William Bowser). Throughout the 1920s, the front page of the Montreal *Gazette* displayed a fascination with American vice and crime, much more so than for signs of Canadian or British depravity.

Myth though it was, the ideal of objectivity enhanced the credibility of the news and thus extended the power of the press. In 1928, George Graham, a journalist and Liberal Senator, claimed that "the impersonal character of Canadian journalism had been its strength."[10] Reporters were able to confer prestige upon individuals. One such media star was no less than Prince Edward, whose tour of Canada in 1919 was so closely covered by the press that he became a popular hero in many a household. Reporters could just as easily destroy reputations, which accounts for the hostility City Hall meted out to the too inquisitive. The careful surveillance the Toronto *Telegram* exercised over civic affairs inspired sufficient fear among local politicians and sufficient admiration among ratepayers to give that paper considerable clout in municipal politics. Newspaper crusades sometimes had dramatic effects. The jingoistic campaign launched by the Montreal *Star* in the fall of 1899, a campaign echoed by much of the anglophone and Conservative press, influenced Laurier's decision to allow Canadian participation in the Boer War. Perhaps of greatest significance was the way in which the press could sway the mood of the public. The shallow optimism that prevailed throughout the middle and later twenties amongst comfortable Canadians was linked to the press focus upon economic expansion and the trivia of life, plus the press neglect of social distress and the troubles of the countryside. News, in short, had become the major kind of common knowledge, at least in urban Canada. News could set the tone and determine the objects of public concern. Not alone of course, but in conjunction with the perspectives and attitudes already present in the public mind. So the daily press through its news columns, better yet its front pages, routinely exercised the awesome powers of recognition and publicity.

A less obvious result of the flood of news, especially the trivia about life, was the decline of the consuming public interest in politics that had been a hallmark of Victorian Canada. This change in the public's perception of what was significant, though, had even more to do with the expansion of the particular offerings for the family, women, and men after 1900. Paradoxically, these offerings both broadened the horizons of readers and focussed their attention upon the little happenings of special worlds. Or again, in a philosophical vein, these offerings contributed to a wider understanding but also a fragmentation of the human experience.

Material designed for a family audience was scattered throughout newspapers, especially in the weekend editions. Some dailies published an actual family page: note, for example, "The Home Page" of the St. John *Telegraph* (1 May, 1930) where a reader could find a serial novel ("The Benson Murder Case" by S. S. Van Dine), one of the "Burgess Bedtime Stories," bridge and home economics lessons, some medical advice, the daily radio programme, and a cartoon ("Our Boarding House"). Beyond this, newspapers supplied round-ups of movies, motoring, boating, and other popular recreations plus reviews of books, music, and theatre for the more cultured. The Saturday editions carried popular science articles, historical tales, brief biographies, notes on exotic lands, and the like for weekend entertainment — so *L'Événement* (22 June, 1929) published "Les Vanderbilts" on a branch of the American plutocracy; "L'Événement historique," this time considering the destruction of Sodom and Gommorah; and "Exploits et aventures," which outlined the life of that Asian scourge, Tamerlane. And not to be forgotten were the comic strips, a page during the week and sometimes four or five pages on the weekend by the end of the 1920s. Indeed, the comics were regarded by the publishers of afternoon or evening dailies as essential features for a mass audience, not just children, and these publishers paid high prices to American syndicates to acquire the exclusive rights to a celebrated strip. A very superficial survey of the family offerings suggests they lacked any particular message, other than a simple-minded enthusiasm for domestic bliss. They were service features which might entertain or divert people as well as provide information to help them enjoy life — whether through radio-listening, movie-going, or outdoor recreation.

The women's pages, sometimes entitled "Le Royaume des Femmes" in Québec dailies, were a more coherent and specialized department. It was aimed principally at the ordinary housewife and mother, though it did appeal to any teenage or adult female whatever her class. On these pages were collected high society news, fashion reports, homemaking hints, perhaps a column on life from a woman's perspective, and even advice for the lovelorn or distressed. Prior to the war, *La Presse* began to publish "Le Courrier de Collette" made up of reader's letters and "Collette's" answers about life's ways, apparently a very successful feature soon emulated by other popular francophone dailies. The women's department, then, might range over many subjects and much of the globe. But such surveillance was always predicated upon the assumption that there was a woman's sphere with a routine and a rhythm quite distinct from the concerns of society at large. Thus was perpetuated that Victorian myth of the separate natures of the sexes.

Men were honoured with two specialized departments, business and sports. For a time, it had seemed there would be a third —labour. Around 1900, a fair number of dailies, especially those with radical proclivities, regularly carried columns of workingman's news and comment. Such comment could be surprisingly frank, as in the case of G. W. Patterson's labour columns in the Saturday edition of the Ottawa Journal.[11] But by the 1920s, this offering had either been dropped or limited to a few paragraphs in much of the press, a change that reflected the middlebrow orientation and conformist bias of the postwar newspaper. First in repute now were the business pages with their focus on finance, local and international markets, and the affairs of big business. Especially impressive was the business department of the Montreal Gazette: on 23 March, 1921, for instance, it covered stock and commodity prices throughout North America, reported on specific events (like the condition of the Bank of Hamilton), and carried little squibs of useful information (such as "VIEWS FROM WALL STREET," the assorted predictions of brokers). First in popularity were the sports pages which divided their attention between a coverage of local and international, amateur and professional sports. Typical was the extensive sports department, roughly three pages, in the Montreal Star (1 September, 1925): a list of tomorrow's entries in the horse races; a roundup of golf activities; items on the amateur sports scene — yachting, swimming, rowing, and tennis; above all, news and analysis of pro sports, from British soccer and cricket to American football and baseball (complete with some obligatory musing about the greatest star of them all, Babe Ruth). Absent here, but common in season, this department gave much attention to the careers of local semi-pro and professional teams in their battles for league supremacy.

What is so striking is the similarity of the business and sports worlds the press surveyed. The two departments boosted their separate pursuits — they thrilled with a sense of the drama and excitement and significance of the little doings of these worlds, never troubling to criticize or question. Both sanctified the "manly" zeal for competition, the business pages with their cult of free enterprise and money-making and the sports pages with their glorification of a ritualized, bloodless combat. They served the active participant yet conveyed an impression of a grand spectacle. The business pages provided the information necessary to the potential investor, as well as an overview of the ups and downs of business affairs for every interested soul. The sports pages notified the athlete, the spectator, and the bettor of the events they might enjoy, while keeping the general public abreast of the whole sports scene. Both departments had a wide purview which extended far beyond the bounds of the locality — the financial reports covering the New York stock exchange and the London money markets and the pro sports review reporting on British soccer or American boxing. And each boasted their own heroes, the captains of industry and the greats of professional sports, The press had thereby manufactured a new type — the "fan" of money-making and sports. Once, indeed as late as the 1880s, business and sports were still very much the preserve of the "classes." But the press had popularized and promoted these kindred worlds, opening them to the eyes of the "masses". If politics and religion had been the enthusiasms of men in the nineteenth century, then business and sports were their counterparts in the twentieth century.

Next in order of importance was the transformation of the advertising the daily carried. Although advertisers used a variety of media, notably packaging, catalogues, magazines, and eventually billboards, the mass newspaper was the prime showcase of North American abundance. The volume of advertising, of course, increased in accord with the size of the daily. As before Confederation, up to two-thirds of the newspaper's contents was advertising matter, sometimes more in the evening dailies with their pages of classifieds and display ads. Likewise, the kinds of products advertised multiplied, the factories of North America turning out an ever greater wealth of goods for the swelling ranks of the comfortable middle class in the cities. But the key change was in the style of advertising. Beginning in the 1890s, advertising was reworked into a sophisticated art of persuasion. Admittedly, the new style could be traced back to the anonymous authors of the outlandish spiels common in patent medicine testimonials. What promoted the new style, though, were the efforts of the copywriters, soon the advertising agencies, who emerged as distinct professionals near the end of the nineteenth century. Under their guidance, newspaper advertising experimented with format, pictures and later photographs, sometimes colour, and always language in order to win the attention of the consumer. The new style, in particular, emphasized product performance over product character. Most important, this style endeavoured to create a desire to consume, rather than merely to inform the public of the wares available.

So began the great age of consumer advertising. For a time, especially in the 1890s and early 1900s, patent medicine ads boomed. Aside from the traditional promises of good health made by concoctions like "South American Nervine Tonic" or "Pink Pills for Pale People," there were direct appeals to men to purchase electrical and magnetic belts that would revitalize their bodily energies (and, by implication, their sex lives) and to women to purchase special powders or liquids that would ease feminine ills, namely the problems associated with menstruation. More lucrative to the publishers were the full-page ads for department stores which soon graced the back pages of the sections of a newspaper. These display ads not only brought in much revenue but actually sold papers, so eager were women to find the latest bargains. And in addition arrived a host of brand name ads: first for soaps like "Pears" or teas like "Salada", but before long for clothes, household appliances, automobiles, cigarettes, hygenic and cosmetic products. Manufacturers hoped thereby to create a public demand so great that merchants would be forced to stock the products advertised. The technique worked. Sometime early in the new century, consumer advertising became the central force in the marketplace. This advertising created within the urban public a willingness to consume well above the need to satisfy basic requirements of life. It enhanced the speed at which new goods were diffused amongst that public. Its impact on the level of demand led entrepreneurs to invest in new kinds of products, to vary and differentiate their products, and to cheapen their products to reach a wider market. The daily newspaper, and the press generally, had become the essential associate of mass consumption and mass production.

If advertising could sell products, why not ideas? Propaganda advertising assumed a major importance only around the time of the Great War. Its sudden prominence had much to do with the efforts of the Canadian Press Association, especially that organization's energetic secretary John W. Imrie. In 1911-12, the CPA endeavoured to boost newspaper profits by mounting a cross-Canada press campaign to promote the idea of advertising to hitherto reluctant businessmen. More spectacular were the results of Imrie's efforts in 1914 to get the government to use the press to mobilize the country for war. Thereafter followed a flood of ads to boost morale ("Good Cheer" messages they were called), to inspire thrift and saving, to purchase victory bonds and so on, in order to foster or rather emphasize those ideas of togetherness and sacrifice necessary to the government's war effort. So successful did this government advertising appear that other special interests turned to the press to promote their causes. During the Winnipeg General Strike of 1919, the Citizen's Committee used full-page ads, filled with vitriol for aliens and reds, to sell the idea of public order, and thus repression, to the respectable citizenry. Prohibitionists and "moderationists" duelled in the press with ads to promote either a dry, and hence, moral Canada or a happy, and hence, slightly wet Canada. Political parties filled papers at election time with their reports of work done (or undone) and promises of the good life ahead under the right government. Business interests, though, were the most consistent users of propaganda advertising. They endeavoured to create public goodwill, either toward business in general or a specific industry. Dating back at least to 1908 were the famous "Made in Canada" campaigns the CMA mounted to promote the consumption of native goods. More localized was the advertising campaign of Vancouver's "White Laundries" which tried via racist appeals to persuade housewives to cease their patronage of the rival Chinese establishments. Many large corporations, such as that natural monopoly Mother Bell, employed what came to be called institutional ads to sell the public upon the notion that the company was motivated by the highest ideals of public service. By and large, then, propaganda advertising worked on the side of the big battalions — the people with sufficient money to purchase newspaper space. Whatever its overall significance, this kind of advertising was usually another weapon in the hands of Canada's establishment.

The most unfortunate change in the daily press was the decline in the quality of argument displayed on the once sacrosanct editorial page. There was, admittedly, a good deal of resistance amongst journalists to any tampering with what tradition declared must be the splendour of the newspaper. As late as 1900, the commentary of the party newspapers remained a proud offering. The practice of stimulating, intelligent argument persisted well into the new century on the editorial pages of leading newspapers like Willison's *News*, Bourassa's *Le Devoir*, and J. W. Dafoe's *Manitoba Free Press*, all editors for whom the chief attraction of journalism was the joy of unrestrained debate. The reputation of Dafoe's editorial page inspired Frank Underhill in 1932 to declare "the Winnipeg *Free Press* is the only newspaper in Canada which exercises anything approaching to a national influence."[12] Besides, the rhetoric of the profession always insisted the editorial page was the soul of the newspaper, the place where a paper applied its wisdom and views to the issues of the day.

This aside, most publishers had broken with past practice in order to fashion an editorial page that would sway the hearts and minds of the masses. The reaction against "the long-winded and patience-wearing"[13] leader had set in soon after Confederation as a result of the successful challenge of people's journalism. Dailies like the Montreal *Star* and the Toronto *Telegram* carried short, snappy editorials, full of colourful language and simple slogans. That was just the beginning of the sacrilege. During the early 1880s, E. E. Sheppard of the Toronto *News* discarded the normal paragraph style of editorials, adopting instead the New York format of disjointed sentences and lavish white space. Around 1900, the Halifax *Echo*, then emphatically a lowbrow sheet, sometimes dropped editorials altogether, making do with short squibs of comment and dry homilies on life. In the first decade of the new century, Joe Atkinson's editors on the Toronto *Star* developed a style of homely argument that spoke to the little man in his own parlance. By the 1920s, though, the editorial pages of the mass dailies had been standardized. The preachy tone, the convoluted argument, the verbal diarrhoea that afflicted the Victorian leader at its worst was gone. So too, unhappily, was the grace, wit, vigour, and scholarship of the leader at its best. If more reasonable, more tolerant, the new-style editorial was usually abbreviated, often bland, a collection of cant and cliché. In particular, it lacked the stamp of a vigorous, committed personality. There might be a few newspapers, mostly morning dailies, which could boast an editorial page of some distinction. But, overall, the editorial page had been humbled.

Not that eccentric comment had disappeared. That became the forte of the resident columnist. In the early 1900s, Toronto's *Mail and Empire* used one "Flaneur" to reflect, from a conservative standpoint, upon the foibles and mores of the age. By contrast, the rival *Star* enjoyed the services of Mrs. Atkinson, a first-class women's columnist who wrote on all manner of subjects under the pseudonym Madge Merton. Indeed, Joe Atkinson was quick to perceive the utility of special columnists. For a time, he employed Harry Gadsby, the vicious and witty Liberal commentator who reached the peak of his fame during the war years. During the 1920s, Atkinson gave free reign to two exotic reverends, R. E. Knowles and Salem Bland. Knowles wrote feature articles and interviews that expressed his own peculiar thoughts on civilization; Bland, a Christian socialist, contributed columns on social questions that eventually earned him obloquy as a "red." These writers enhanced the notoriety of the *Star*. The columnist might specialize in humour or politics, pessimism or dissent. No matter — his comments added colour to the daily offerings, and pleased loyal readers, but without committing the newspaper itself. So the daily could become a forum for idiosyncratic views that might explore the odd corners of life, boom unpopular causes, or even clash with official editorial policy.

The power of the press did not suffer. True, people might not read editorials with the same avid devotion as their grandparents. Only in moments of great excitement, such as a major strike or a political crisis, did readers turn eagerly to the editorial page for explanations. Otherwise the comics, sad to say, were a much more popular item. Nonetheless, the editorial page, the regular columns of comment, and the headlined news had become the leading instruments of mass propaganda in Canada's political democracy. Nothing compared with the huge audience the daily press could command for its opinions. That accounts for the concern politicians and businessmen evinced over the contents of the editorial page. The assumption editorials could influence scads of people affected the judgements, the decisions of the establishment. That influence might be a myth, but the myth itself could only enhance the significance of the press. Besides, the very homeliness of the new-style editorial made it an effective agent of persuasion for a mass audience. The lack of sophistication of the average reader suggests this audience was more susceptible to persuasion: if not directly through editorials, then indirectly via the news. Ironically, the waning interest in public affairs, and so lessened strength of existing attitudes, likely increased the dependence of the public upon the opinions served up by the press. The views of the mass newspapers, in short, had a greater impact upon the outlook of their times than the perfervid arguments of their colonial ancestors had ever enjoyed in their day.

IV

The transformation of big city journalism, peculiar as it may seem, first widened and then severely narrowed the intellectual horizons of the press. Certain patterns of ideas, certain kinds of attitudes, of course, remained constant. The parochialism of the press was unshaken. The newspaper was first a local medium that usually reflected, and favoured, the interests of its immediate constituency. That reflex assumed a particular importance in controversies over race and religion, or the merits of a provincial rights campaign, or the justice of farm grievances. During the 1880s, for instance, John Ross Robertson's *Telegram* lambasted greedy farmers, Ottawa politicians, French and Catholic conspirators, all of whom apparently hindered efforts to remake the nation in Toronto's image. This kind of parochialism was checked by a varying loyalty to a party credo. Normally, the press echoed the Conservative and Liberal emphasis upon the maintenance of the Canadian union. Though invariably a zealous champion of the rights of French Canada, often critical of anglophone nativists, and imperialists, *La Presse* never doubted the wisdom of Confederation, even during the harrowing years of the Great War. Likewise, newspapers subsumed parochial differences in the grander controversies that troubled the minds of party leaders. Those often tedious disputes over the protective tariff and the nation's destiny pervaded the editorial pages of the whole period. The Liberal *Manitoba Free Press* was still fighting the same battle for a freer trade and a more independent Canada in 1925 as it had in 1905. So, too, the usually Conservative Montreal *Star* sang the praises of industrial protection and Imperial unity for over forty years. What united the press was, as before Confederation, a commitment to the reigning social orthodoxy — that ubiquitous bourgeois ethos. Even the people's journals of the late nineteenth century acted as the publicists of this ethos. In particular, the press fixed the identity of the Dominion as a Victorian commonwealth, a land of economic progress and ordered liberty, of moral rectitude and hard work, of class harmony and happy families. Therein lay the source of that sense of moral superiority with which native-born Canadians viewed their nation and their world, and notably their American neighbours.

By far the most fascinating phenomenon was the re-emergence of a native radicalism. Its revival and its persistence resulted from the social tensions generated by industrialism, especially in the cities. Not to be discounted, either, was the influence of American Populist and later Progressive rhetoric, although Canadian radicalism was not a mere imitation of any American movement. The radical perspective was born anew in the iconoclastic enthusiasms of the people's journals. Almost immediately though, their chant was taken up by assorted Liberal newspapers, in particular the discernably rouge *La Patrie* and the slightly proletarian Victoria *Times*. By the Laurier years, the radical perspective counted sufficient press champions to win recognition by contemporaries as a third force in public debate. Not only popular dailies like the two Montréal giants, the *Star* and *La Presse*, but even more reserved newspapers such as the Winnipeg *Tribune* and the Ottawa *Citizen* voiced radical concerns. Toronto, alone, had three radical advocates: the *Star*, the *Telegram*, and the *World*. Throughout the press, of course, radical dailies were never as numerous as their liberal and conservative rivals. Always there were more voices praising than criticizing the status quo; indeed they were fearful that radical measures would undermine national prosperity or dispossess the propertied classes or open the way to social revolution. Still, the early 1900s was one of the few times in the Canadian past when radical ideas could justly claim a wide currency, indeed command respectability.

What underlay this radicalism was a deep sympathy for the underdog. The perspective itself rested upon a simple, moral conception of the community, in which the "classes" were all too often evil and the "masses" usually good. That assumption inspired a muckraking zeal: the radical was ever in search of some conspiracy against the public good, whether among arrogant politicians or greedy monopolists. A hallmark of radicalism was the crusade, so effective a method of pinpointing an injustice and exciting public indignation. The *La Presse* exposé in 1886 of "un job de $37,000," growing out of a paving contract for the city of Montréal and suggestions of aldermanic impropriety, was typical. Implicit in radical rhetoric was the ideal of a triumphant democracy wherein the common man might stand free and proud. That found expression in the early demand for manhood suffrage, a disdain for social convention and snobbery, sometimes a suspicion of moral reform, and the innumerable campaigns against business exploitation. A specific instance was the support the Montreal *Star* and the Hamilton *Herald* gave around 1890 to the single-tax panacea of Henry George, hoping that a readjustment of property taxes in the city would relieve the burdens of the lowly taxpayer. Undeniably, the new radicalism was diffuse, lacking any theoretical rigour and so subject to eccentric definition. One of the weirdest varieties was the democratic republicanism in the mid-1880s of E. E. Sheppard's Toronto *News*, an unashamed advocate of the total Americanization of the Dominion. Numbered among the leaders in the radical press during the Laurier years was a tory populist (Robertson's *Telegram*), a public ownership fanatic (Billy Maclean's *World*), a timid social democrat (Atkinson's *Star*), and an agrarian rebel (R. L. Richardson's *Tribune*). Furthermore, the radical fervour of these newspapers had definite limits, not the least being its superficiality. The effusive sympathy *La Presse* displayed for the workingman and the poor was always seconded to a loyalty to its party masters. Besides, every radical assumed the virtues of the bourgeois ethos, in particular the growth ethic and the myth of class harmony. No wonder a cynic might think the radical message was spiced with a large dose of opportunism, merely another technique publishers used to drum up additional circulation.

Even so, the radical dailies were the foremost publicists of reform. At bottom, their message amounted to a plea for the modernization of Canadian attitudes and institutions to meet the ills of the new urban nation. From the beginning, the people's journals championed what was called "the march of labour." Their columns of trade union news, their editorial support of laws to protect the labourer's wages or lessen his hours, their attack upon business exploitation, all publicized and so justified the workingman's demand for a square deal. Carrying that campaign into the new century, Atkinson's *Star* won many laurels as the most stalwart defender of labour's rights, notably the right to collective bargaining. Perhaps the paper's greatest moment came in 1919 when it displayed, almost alone among daily newspapers, a sympathy for the cause of the Winnipeg strikers. In any case, papers like the *Star* made respectable the whole idea of trade unionism, much to the consternation of many a businessman. No less important, the radical press called upon the state to take command of the industrial economy, in particular to discipline big business. Its voice fostered that extraordinary surge of interest amongst the populace in the technique of public ownership of civic utilities, electrical power, even telephones and railways. The Ontario campaign for public hydro took on the guise of a holy crusade for economic progress, social justice, and political democracy in the news and editorial pages of the radical press, especially the Toronto *World*. Public opinion was so effectively mobilized that Adam Beck, the head of Ontario Hydro, was unbeatable and uncontrolled. More prosaic but still laudable were the successes the radical press scored in the ongoing battle to save the Canadian city. The crusades of these newspapers initiated efforts to reform municipal government, to organize an efficient civic bureaucracy, to improve public health and welfare services and to plan the city's growth. Toronto's reputation as the most enlightened city in Canada had much to do with the vigour and power of its three radical dailies. But the chief legacy of the radical press was in the realm of ideas: its articulation of a concept of the public interest, superior to any vested interests, that justified the state's intervention in private affairs to protect and benefit the community. The radical dailies were the first heralds of that collectivist impulse which would grow ever stronger in later years.

The last efflorescence of radicalism was the postwar reconstruction fad, a peculiar outburst of press and public support for a reformed democracy that might justify the sacrifices of the Great War. The day of reform, however, had passed: partly the red scare, the fear of Bolshevism abroad and at home, but more the apparent satisfaction of the bourgeois citizenry with their lot contributed to a definite rightward swing in press opinion during the course of the 1920s. The Progressive party which burst into political prominence after the election of 1921 might have enjoyed the enthusiastic support of rural Canada but it found little welcome in urban Canada, even among the erstwhile champions of radicalism. A few newspapers kept the old faith. The Southam's Citizen, soon referred to as "that screwy paper in Ottawa,"[14] not only supported the Progressives but later picked up the eccentric idea of Social Credit. Atkinson's Star, also sympathetic to the Progressives, continued to espouse the virtues of a social liberalism attuned to the needs of the little man, but without the same sense of urgency as in times past. Otherwise, one radical after another embraced the new mood of anxious conformity. Hugh Graham's Montreal Star, if still grumpy, was also decidedly reactionary. The tory populism of the Toronto Telegram became more and more a memory, now that John Ross Robertson was dead. Too often, the Winnipeg Tribune, a new part of the Southam chain, contented itself with boosting the glorious potential of Winnipeg. Indeed, dailies everywhere were the fervent adherents of the cult of community service, which usually meant an automatic support of whatever projects the local establishment might deem wise. No wonder the editorial pages of the mass press seemed bland and tiresome. The press was again, by and large, the voice of conventional wisdom.

The death of radicalism was linked to the place of the mass press within the complex of Canada's social institutions. Over the years, the much touted independence of the press began to acquire some substance. The economics of daily journalism lessened the newspaper's reliance upon the monies and influence of outsiders and worked against the survival of the once common organ. Publishers came to recognize their profits rested more upon the public's patronage than anything else. Perhaps the churches suffered most. Their influence over press behaviour waned rapidly, even before the turn of the century. Not only because of the disappearance of the sectarian journal, but because the race for circulation destroyed the newspaper as an effective agent of Christian morality. La Presse or the Toronto Star, though never antireligious, specialized in the coverage of secular life, often the seamy side of life. As early as 1896, A. T. Drummond feared "the chronicling of crime forms, in fact, such a feature in the modern newspaper that we are apt to assume that the world is becoming morally worse, instead of better, under the influence of Christianity."[15] What meaning could God have in a world defined by the trivia of the police court, high society, the sports arena, or the stock exchange? The new religion amounted to a gospel of consumption preached by the advertising pages. Of course, the mass daily always boosted the moral authority of the churches over the social mores of the people. Indeed, La Presse was effusively pious, ever ready to open its columns to a bishop or to praise the teachings of the Catholic church. The daily press was an unconscious instrument of secularization because the very volume and extent of its communications undermined the perception of the sacred in daily life.

Much more slowly, the parties lost their stranglehold upon the press. The first symptom of this change was the commercial success of the people's journals, which mirrored the passions and prejudices of their readers as much as the views of a party. Worse, at least from a Conservative standpoint, was the failure of two advocates, the Toronto *Empire* in 1895 and *Le Journal* a decade later, which had proved too costly to keep afloat. Even before the Great War, the supposedly Conservative Southam chain began to break down into a collection of newspapers favouring different views in accord with their publishers' whims. The political trauma of 1917 shattered the unity of the Liberal press in English Canada: dailies as prominent as the Toronto *Globe*, the Toronto *Star*, and the *Manitoba Free Press* broke ranks to support conscription and Union government in the ensuing election. Especially symbolic was the refusal of "CP" in 1923 to grant a news franchise to a planned Ottawa daily desired by no less than Mackenzie King. Not even Liberal publishers would back the launching of this newcomer in an already rationalized market. By the Depression, newspapers normally avoided a blatant partisanship because it might offend some readers and thus threaten profits. In French Québec, Pamphile DuTremblay and Jacob Nicol, two Liberal partisans who controlled much of the daily press,[16] neutered the news and moderated the opinions of their newspapers after the victory of Maurice Duplessis in 1936. At election time, newspapers often kept their editorial pages reasonable, leaving the old-fashioned rhetoric to paid political advertisements. In ordinary times, the more secure felt free to criticize party leaders whenever they departed from right principles. In fact, during the mid-1920s, the Toronto *Globe* solemnly announced its disenchantment with certain policies of the King government. The party organ was fast becoming an anachronism in Canada.

Even so, newspapers were rarely neutral in the political fray. Their publishers were often partisans in their own right, who enjoyed playing politics almost as much as their colonial predecessors. Between 1918 and 1924, G. Fred Pearson of the Halifax *Chronicle* maintained a close correspondence with W. S. Fielding, Nova Scotia's great Liberal politician. Not only did the two men exchange views on political issues, they consulted on party matters (notably partisan appointments) and the line the *Chronicle* should take in assorted controversies. It was so very reminiscent of the grand tradition of nineteenth century political journalism. The spoils of victory might be more honorary than monetary, but still worthwhile. Amongst those publishers called to the Senate were William Templeman of the Victoria *Times* (1897), Robert

Jaffray of the Toronto *Globe* (1906), William Dennis of the Halifax *Herald* (1912), Richard Smeaton White of the Montreal *Gazette* (1917), W. A. Buchanan of the Lethbridge *Herald* (1925), William Henry Dennis of the Halifax *Herald* (1932), Pamphile DuTremblay of *La Presse* (1942), and Jacob Nicol of *Le Soleil* (1944). One publisher, Walter Nichol of the Vancouver *Province*, was chosen Lieutenant-Governor of British Columbia in 1920. Hugh Graham not only received a knighthood but eventually a peerage, becoming Lord Atholstan in 1917. Out of habit or conviction, a newspaper usually favoured one party, at least on its editorial pages. That was expected. A reader in 1930 could easily identify the Liberal sympathies of the Halifax *Chronicle*, the Toronto *Globe*, or the Victoria *Times* and the Conservative bias of the Halifax *Herald*, the Toronto *Mail and Empire*, or the Victoria *Colonist*. The party press lived on, if more the associate than the servant of the party leader.

Some critics, as early as the 1880s, charged that the press was merely exchanging the yoke of big business for the rule of party. That worry arose, in part, out of the investments the Canadian Pacific Railway made in the press to ensure a favourable treatment. In particular, the company managed to buy off two Liberal critics, the Montreal *Herald* in the mid-1880s and the *Manitoba Free Press* at the end of the decade. Equally worrisome were the connections individual capitalists established with newspapers. In 1895, Frederic Nicholls, an industrialist, purchased the Toronto *Star* to fight for unbounded free enterprise and private property. In 1902, James Dunsmuir, always a coal baron but then also provincial premier, acquired full control of the Victoria *Colonist* whose reactionary opinions had already earned it the nickname the "daily Dunsmuir."[17] Perhaps the most notorious incident was the *La Presse* affair of 1904: secretly, a syndicate of anglophone capitalists (including Hugh Graham of the Montreal *Star*) bought the newspaper for $750,000 in order to vilify, hopefully upset, the Laurier government and so forward various railway and political schemes. The plot collapsed once the story leaked out and before long the newspaper had been returned into the hands of a penitent Trefflé Berthiaume. That episode illustrated the limits of big business influence over the press. As soon as a newspaper earned a reputation as a purchased organ of big business, its public significance and even circulation was likely to suffer. Besides, most businessmen were not interested in a consistent organ, only in a purchase of news and editorial columns to boom some crotchet or project. The CPR eventually relinquished its newspaper properties. The group of business stars (including Timothy Eaton and Peter Larkin) who, on behalf of the Liberal party, had invested in a refurbished Toronto *Star* in 1899 slowly sold their shares to Joe Atkinson. The man that bankrolled the Vancouver *Sun* during the Great War, one Colonel J. W. Stewart who thought he needed a newspaper to support his railway interests, did in time turn over the property to its publisher, R. J. Cromie. On the whole, then, financiers, industrialists, railwaymen, and the like did not endeavour to take direct command of the daily press.

In fact, the business community was usually well-served by the press, even when newspaper radicalism was in flower. True, certain kinds of enterprises, notably civic utilities, did receive much abuse because of their unpopularity amongst the public. Likewise, the occasional capitalist, say Joseph Flavelle of bacon fame at the end of the war, was pilloried for excessive greed. But the cause of business, in general, had many admirers. Partly, that was because of the importance of advertising to the survival and profit of the newspaper. Not that a publisher was necessarily subservient to an individual advertiser: in 1921, Atkinson successfully defied Sir John Eaton, a very important patron, who protested "the Bolshevistic trend" of the Star.[18] Rather, the big city newspaper was less likely to condemn, much more likely to praise, the business tycoons whose revenue made it prosperous — a complaint sounded on occasion by small retailers and labour leaders. Just as important were the interests and assumptions of the publishers of the dailies. Leading publishing families like the Riordons of the Toronto Mail, later Mail and Empire (1877-1927), the Jaffrays of the Toronto Globe (1888-1936), or the Siftons of the Manitoba Free Press (1898 onwards) had extensive interests in other kinds of enterprises. W. Sandford Evans, owner of the Winnipeg Telegram, was a leading force in the city's commercial elite, and sufficiently prominent to win the mayoralty in 1909. The Spencer family that had made good in the department store business gained control of William Templeman's once radical Victoria Times, after his death in 1914. The Southams' investment in the private Cataract Power Company apparently conditioned the Hamilton Spectator's long opposition to the idea and the reality of Ontario Hydro. Perhaps most suggestive, though, is an anecdote about B. F. Pearson and Max Aitken. Pearson, owner of the Halifax Chronicle, was a lawyer and company promoter involved in a variety of Nova Scotian enterprises and Mexican utilities. In 1911, the Chronicle joined in the general Liberal attack upon Aitken, an even greater promoter but also a Conservative then under a cloud. Aitken wrote to Pearson pointing out, "You and I have both been concerned in the creation of watered capital."[19] Pearson admitted the error of his paper's ways, blaming an editor for the unwarranted criticism. Harmony was restored. The moral of the story? — namely, that the masters of the press were often members of the wider community of big business that had matured by the Great War.

The most striking evidence of the new autonomy of the press was the prominence of the "paper tyrant,"[20] the publisher who sought to advance his own ambitions or causes in public life. During the late 1880s, the mysterious Charles Riordon allowed his once Conservative Toronto *Mail* to espouse both an Anglo-Protestant ascendancy and a commercial union with the United States in an effort to work a political revolution in Canada. In the mid-1900s, Joseph Flavelle hoped the rhetoric of the independent Toronto *News* would somehow inspire the purification of public debate and political life. Billy Maclean employed the Toronto *World* to challenge Robert Borden's leadership of the Conservative opposition. Henri Bourassa intended that *Le Devoir* would break the grip Laurier, in particular, and party politicians, in general, had upon the minds of the electorate. Hugh Graham of the Montreal *Star* (Canada's closest equivalent to William Randolph Hearst) used his reputed influence and real wealth to interfere constantly in the affairs of the Québec wing of the Conservative party — causing Borden and later Arthur Meighen a good deal of trouble. The most feared paper tyrant, however, was Joe Atkinson. Just after the Great War, one commentator called him "the most dangerous force in Canadian journalism today," because his *Star* apparently ruled the minds of so many ordinary people.[21] In truth, following 1917, Atkinson did try to exercise his power to advance his vision of a radical democracy. He soon failed. Atkinson's return to the Liberal fold by the mid-1920s demonstrated that the power of the paper tyrant was more myth than reality. No publisher could transform his supposed sway over the public mind into an independent political force. The inertia of the political system was just too great to allow a publisher to realize his personal dreams. The wise man, and Atkinson was certainly wise, recognized he must work in association with some party.

V

This truism, however, should not mask the fact that the rise of the big dailies, less so the consumer magazines and the nationwide class journals, had worked something of a revolution in Canadian ideas. Canada's first mass media were, by persuasion but even more by nature, the spokesmen of democracy. First the people's journals, soon after the party press, endorsed the principles of political democracy. By the 1890s, the press had begun to purvey that cult of the common man which would eventually attain a high place in the pantheon of Canadian orthodoxy. The dreams, the fears, the beliefs, the decisions of this mythical common man were glorified everywhere in print. News columns opened much of society, from the boardrooms of business to the slums of the city, to his eyes. Advertising sanctified his tastes, the special departments reinforced his passions, and the editorials flattered his wisdom. How typical of the temper of the times was the offhand comment of the Vancouver *Sun* (26 November, 1920): "the composite public mind," thought its editorial writer, was "keen, judicial, and in the long run always fair." Public opinion reigned supreme, it would seem, not only in politics, but over the economy, the culture, and the society.

This public opinion, of course, was emphatically bourgeois and urban. What the daily newspapers and the consumer magazines did was to alter and standardize, even more to popularize the mores of the urban middle class. Bourgeois organizations, from the boards of trade to the associated charities, received the sympathetic attention of the news columns of the dailies. Better yet, the values and causes of this class were advanced by the press. Take the example of the growth ethic. During the 1870s, the Conservative press mounted a massive propaganda campaign on behalf of a protective tariff to convince the public of the virtues of a "Big Canada" committed to industrial growth. By the end of the century, the myth of industrial self-sufficiency had become a part of the conventional wisdom of the urban public. After 1900, the mass press boomed the optimism of "Canada's century" and an intolerance toward its builders. Both were evident in the rhetoric of J. W. Dafoe's *Free Press*, which first welcomed the European immigrants for what they could make of the virgin prairie, but by the end of the war feared these aliens for what insidious influences they might fix in the Canadian milieu. Similarly, the same press championed the vaunting ambitions of a middle class eager to engineer a better Canada. During the late nineteenth century, big city dailies demanded the modernization of the assorted social authorities that were supposed to civilize the country. Some anglophone dailies, for instance, criticized the persistence of denominational differences amongst the Protestant churches and called for a common Christian front to strengthen the moral character of the unruly cities — a forerunner of the social gospel. Later on, that mood took a more concrete form in the upsurge of urban progressivism fostered by the radical newspapers. In prewar Ontario, Atkinson's *Star* exhibited a puritanical longing for moral regulation that would limit booze and save the Christian Sabbath, as well as a reformist zeal for urban improvement that would make Toronto a healthy, well-run, equitable city. Even the francophone press was affected: Bourassa's *Le Devoir* favoured both social reform and moral rearmament to bolster the Catholic ways of an industrializing Québec. The apparent success of the middle class by the 1920s was reflected in the Babbittry and conformity of the daily press. It was a time to chronicle and celebrate the Canadian achievement, perhaps to defend that achievement from social revolution through publications as diverse as *Saturday Night* and the Montreal *Star*, but not a time to change that achievement.

The working people, in particular, suffered the ill effects of this class bias. Artisans, perhaps labourers as well, had survived the nineteenth century with distinctive traditions of work and life — the concept of a living wage, a belief in workshop autonomy, various rituals and holidays, above all a proud sense of identity. The climate of opinion, though, was hardly congenial to the rise of a coherent, self-conscious, or powerful working class. The mass press popularized an entrepreneurial ideal that glorified the businessman as a national hero, acquisition as a public good, and competition as a progressive force. Time and again, this press urged the virtues of industrial harmony, ever ready to call upon the state to impose peace upon a warring Capital and Labour, an action usually against the best interests of the workingman. Even the radical perspective that certain dailies advanced blunted the workingman's consciousness by subsuming his grievances in the wider challenge of the "masses" against the "classes," and by enlisting his aid for the assorted reforms concocted by bourgeois spokesmen. Certainly, whatever support the radical press might lend trade unionism, its sympathies rarely extended to working class or socialist politics, both a threat to the social order. Beyond this, might it not be true that the workingman was seduced by the happy messages of the daily press? To speculate: his curiosity was satisfied by news trivia, his natural bent toward equality transmuted into an enthusiasm for spectator sports, his sense of identity linked to his ability (often inability) to consume. Now, labour journals and trade unions did work with some success to organize a portion of the skilled work force into a self-conscious interest with a certain clout in the marketplace (less so in the political arena). But the fashioning of a proletarian culture was well-nigh impossible in the pervasive bourgeois milieu of early twentieth century Canada. That may help to explain the decline of the class struggle which reporters saw looming large on the Canadian horizon, especially just at the end of the war. In any case, there was some justice to L'Événement's smug claim (1 May, 1929) that Québec's workingmen were sane and Christian, untainted by the extremism of other lands, committed to the social virtues of the wider community. That stereotype also applied to much of the working class throughout Canada on the eve of the Depression.

The countryfolk were better insulated against the corrosive influences of the mass press. True enough, even before 1900, farm publicists complained that dailies and magazines (along with books and schools) cultivated an impression of the exciting city which pulled the young away to jobs in the professions, business, or the factories. But the countryside boasted its own organs of defence, sometimes convinced Canada was an embattled land wherein city and town, factory and farm, urban dweller and countryfolk waged a struggle for predominance. The small town weeklies were early, if occasional, critics of big city power. During the mid-1890s, for instance, the Regina Standard (echoing the crotchets of American Populists) called for free trade, planned inflation, and an assault upon big banks and big railways to save the Dominion from the horrors of plutocratic rule. Less eccentric, the *Farmers' Sun*, after 1892, and the *Grain Growers' Guide*, after 1908, worked to roll back the clock by reaffirming the primacy of the family farm in the national economy. After the war, the concern that the church magazines displayed over the immoral ways of the city could only nourish the prejudices of their rural readers. Even metropolitan papers, say the *Family Herald and Weekly Star*, defended home and hearth against urban novelty. For rural Canada was a huge, diverse domain with ways and institutions of its own. In the years after Confederation, the countryside expanded into the prairies, threw up a variety of militant organizations, sponsored the Progressive revolt of the early 1920s, and maintained a good deal of its autonomy. So large and vigorous a domain (about half of Canada's population was considered "rural" in 1931) was not likely to fall under the spell of the city or its organs.

All of which suggests there were definite limits to the influence of the mass media. Whatever the importance of these giants, they were a relative novelty, their power checked by tradition, by other institutions, even by the lesser media. The public, in cities as well as the countryside, was still influenced by the loyalties of their parents and grandparents. The school and the church waged a stubborn rearguard action for the minds of the people. Most important, the country press, the class journals, and the like perpetuated the diversity of Canadian life. So the Canada of the 1920s seemed a land of contrasts. On the one hand, an observer might emphasize the consumer boom, the hedonistic mood, the fascination with professional sports, the decline of partisanship, the American style of life. On the other hand, this same observer could find the persistence of the Victorian imprint, the vigour of limited identities, the survival of a puritanical zeal, the health of amateur sports, a deep loyalty to British ways and the British connection in English Canada or a great respect for Catholic dogma and the Catholic church in French Canada. The "modern" had not yet overtaken the "traditional."

The big city dailies and their associates constituted Canada's second mature system of communications. The dailies, in particular, were a complete medium of mass communication. They furnished information and opinion, entertainment and education to a large, heterogeneous public. Their messages had begun to turn popular culture into an artifact of fashion rather than custom. Whatever their origin, and obviously they were rooted in the folkways of the past, the values implicit in these messages acquired an independent existence by the very fact of production for and dissemination to all sorts of people. The enormous popularity of the messages made them an important force in Canadian life, at least among a fair portion of the urban public. Obviously, the press acted as an agent of consensus: the habitual consumption of its messages united people otherwise divided by distance, religion, language, or class. People shared a common idiom. Paradoxically, the press was also an agent of conflict: the same habitual consumption divided people into rival partisans, city boosters, nationalists, or sports fans. The mass media could satisfy both the communal and the bellicose instincts of their readers. That remained more a promise than a reality in early twentieth century Canada, though. Mass communications would not attain a general sway over the public mind, more properly popular culture, until the triumph of the multimedia.

Notes:

1 "The Evening Telegram." A Story of the Years (Toronto, 1889), p. 3.

2 Le Nouveau Monde continued as the Conservative Le Monde (later Le Monde Canadien) until the end of the century; likewise, La Vérité lasted under a different editorship into the 1920s. Other papers that espoused the ultramontane perspective were Le Courrier du Canada (1857-1901), Le Journal de Trois-Rivières (1865-1893), Le Nouvelliste (1876-1886), Le Canadien (only briefly in the late 1870s and early 1880s), and La Justice (1886-1892).

3 All figures are for circulations in 1931.

4 That figure for June of 1930.

5 Circulation figures, 1931: Maclean's Magazine (160,835), Chatelaine (121,760), Canadian Homes and Gardens (7,750?), and Mayfair (10,328).

6 A colleague at the University of Toronto, Michael Bliss, who is preparing a biography of Flavelle, kindly passed on the financial statement of the News for 1907 used in the text.

7 W. D. Lesueur, "The Newspaper Press and the University," Journalism and the University (Toronto: Queen's Quarterly, 1903), p. 255.

8 C. McNaught, Canada Gets the News (Toronto: Ryerson, 1940), p. 16.

9 The Canadian Associated Press, organized by John Ross Robertson of the Toronto Telegram early in the century and supported by other central Canadian dailies, which supplied British and imperial news taken apparently from the British press. It was supported by a federal subsidy, eventually of $8,000 a year.

10 Canadian Annual Review, 1927-28, p. 612. Graham was speaking in opposition to Tommy Church's bill which would have required newspapers to publish the names and holdings of their owners.

11 Patterson was a proofreader in the Government Printing Bureau. His topics included a defence of unionism, investigations of the cost of living, and attacks upon the "trusts."

12 F. Underhill, "J. W. Dafoe," In Search of Canadian Liberalism (Toronto: Macmillan, 1961), p. 141. Reprinted from the Canadian Forum, October, 1932.

13 "The Evening Telegram." A Story of the Years, p. 8.

14 An epithet quoted in Pierre Berton, "The Southams," Maclean's Magazine, 15 June, 1950, p. 66.

15 A. T. Drummond, "Are our American Newspapers Degenerating?," Queen's Quarterly, 3, January 1896, p. 194.

16 Pamphile DuTremblay owned La Presse and La Patrie; Jacob Nicol controlled a network that included Le Soleil and L'Événement-Journal of Québec City, La Tribune of Sherbrooke, and Le Nouvelliste of Trois-Rivières.

17 D. A. McGregor, "Adventures of Vancouver Newspapers: 1892-1926," British Columbia Historical Quarterly, 10, April 1946, p. 99.

18 R. Harkness, J. E. Atkinson of the Star (Toronto: University of Toronto Press, 1963), p. 137.

19 Cited in A. J. P. Taylor's Beaverbrook (London: Hamish Hamilton, 1972), p. 65.

20 The term "paper tyrant" was coined by Ron Poulton in his biography of John Ross Robertson, The Paper Tyrant. John Ross Robertson of the Toronto Telegram (Toronto: Clarke Irwin, 1971.).

21 Harkness, J. E. Atkinson of the Star, p. 116.

III
The Triumph of The Multimedia

Canadians avidly accepted television. In the spring of 1953, sales of television sets in the Toronto area alone were estimated at some thirty thousand a month.[1] The extraordinary advance of television signified the completion of a revolution in communications that has surrounded nearly every person in a blanket of messages. "Television marks the high point of a curve in the development of mass communications," noted Max Rosenfeld, a *Maclean's* writer, in 1954. "Each new medium has tended to embrace a younger group of devotees. Newspapers and magazines, oldest of the four giants of mass communication, are read mainly by adults. Movies have been able to win the adolescents. Next, radio absorbed the preadolescents. With the advent of television, mass communication appears destined to absorb us from the cradle to the grave — television is viewed with rapt attention even by infants."[2]

I

The present-day importance of the multimedia is one consequence of that cardinal attribute of social development in the twentieth century, the rise of mass affluence. Now by "affluence," I mean the money, security, leisure, and freedom sufficient to enjoy North American abundance. While mass affluence may have had its origins in the Laurier years, its values and mores only came to dominate Canadian life in the decades following the close of World War II. The fall in the hours of labour dating from the first decade of the century, the upward march of real wages that began just after the Great War, and the spread of security through union contracts and social welfare schemes following the Depression made ever larger segments of the population affluent. Not all Canadians have won this affluence, of course. In recent years, the expansion of affluence has apparently halted, if not reversed. Still, roughly three-quarters of the population are privileged — mostly unionized blue-collar workers, white collar employees, and their families. So profound is this change that a true definition of citizenship would presuppose affluence. Even the meaning of poverty has been altered: non-affluence, not destitution, is its determining characteristic.

And the reality of affluence has breached the old boundaries of class, creed, language, and location.

Against this background, the phenomenal growth of the new modes of communication followed a common pattern of diffusion and acceptance. Each was greeted with surprise, a sense of wonder that fostered a craze especially amongst the lower stata of the population with whom the older media were never quite in tune. Before long though, the innovation strove for respectability and profit by appealing to the affluent public, so winning status as a necessity rather than a luxury. At first, the novelty of the medium challenged the position of its established rivals, and usually undermined their hold upon the public; but, in time, all adjusted and the newcomer supplemented its brethren, thereby enhancing the sway of mass communications. Indeed, over the years, consumer usage of the mass media, and therefore the profits of the communications industry, have proved resistant to downturns in the economy. The result, notably after the advent of television, was the emergence of the multimedia as a single institution.

First to arrive were the movies, right at the end of the nineteenth century. Although largely an American development, in which Thomas Edison played the major role, the movies immediately crossed the border into Canada, further evidence that the continent was a single market for popular entertainment. The cheap, abbreviated, crude melodramas that the first movies offered appealed to the tastes and the pocketbooks of the semi-literate, in particular immigrant and native working people. Across the face of Canada, mostly urban Canada, spread touring exhibitors, then peep-show parlours, and soon nickelodeons. In 1909, downtown Winnipeg hosted eleven "picture theatres" (as against fifty-one pool rooms and fifty "disorderly houses," the last segregated in a red light district).[3] The older kinds of popular entertainment, namely the cheap theatre and vaudeville, began to hurt from the competition of movies. Already, entrepreneurs in search of greater profits were endeavouring to reach the respectable public — in 1907, L. Ernest Ouimet opened in Montréal a picture palace, grandly called the "Ouimetoscope," with plush accoutrements that emulated the style of the best theatres. Such events won the attention of the daily press, always prepared to serve a new, popular interest. By 1915, for instance, the Montreal Star carried an "At the Movies" column, though its entertainment section still showed more concern with opera, concerts, and the theatre.

The cinema attained the status of a mass medium sometime after the Great War, when the affluent public as a whole became habitual moviegoers. The prime reason for the quick acceptance of movies was the sophistication of the Hollywood product. Beginning just after the war, the development of feature-length movies, a garish style of promotional hype, and the birth of the star system all fueled public interest. Most important, Hollywood was soon producing a plethora of formula melodramas, the famous "B" movies: comedy, war pictures, westerns (and "northerns" set in the Canadian wilderness), gangster and horror flicks, thrillers and adventures. At the end of the decade, when public interest seemed to be flagging because of radio, Hollywood came forth with "talkies" that brought even more people to the cinema. Meanwhile, the industry had been concentrated into a series of interlocking networks of studios, distribution companies, and moviehouses, making the movies a cheap, convenient, and ever pleasing amusement for the masses. By 1930, going to the movies was a common weekly ritual for families in Canada's cities. The Depression did not alter this ritual, though the industry's profits fell in the early 1930s. In 1936, for instance, the country's 956 motion picture theatres earned twenty-nine million dollars from 126 million admissions, a per capita rate of twelve attendances a year. Cheap entertainment was still a must, most especially in hard times.

The heyday of the movies ran from the early 1940s to the mid-1950s. Hollywood, and now European movie centres, supplied a diversity of escapist fare aimed at a mass audience broken up into families, young couples, and children. The musical, in particular, reached its highest expression as an art form. So too, perhaps, did the gangster film. As against these standardized products, the National Film Board distributed to rural Canada, the schools, and voluntary associations a wealth of documentaries. Even the avant-garde cinema entered Canada from Europe with the appearance of film societies in the major cities. Neither the offerings of the NFB nor the film societies, of course, could compete with the spell of the mass cinema. The number of motion picture theatres increased to a high of 1,950 in 1955, as the cinema followed the people into the surburbs. And these moviehouses were supplemented by the teenage "passion pits," some 250 drive-ins (except in Québec where they were banned). Although per capita attendance had peaked at nineteen in 1946, and organized sports as well as family recreations expanded enormously in postwar Canada, moviegoing had remained a central ritual of the affluent life.

Radio was born just as movies matured, in the 1920s. Radio's early growth was chaotic. Unlike Great Britain and the United States, broadcasting in Canada lacked a John Reith or a David Sarnoff to guide its development, though Henry Thornton of the Canadian National Railways did try to give a fillip to quality programming. Because of the nature of radio technology, the federal government assumed the authority to grant licenses and wavelengths to ensure a minimal amount of order. But, otherwise, the state adopted a laissez-faire attitude. Politicians, apparently, thought radio a mere toy, unworthy of a decided policy. The Department of Marine and Fisheries (the licensing agency) granted broadcasting privileges to zealous amateurs, radio set manufacturers, newspapers, the CNR, universities, even religious bodies. Primitive equipment plus shared wavelengths, in addition to growing American competition on the airwaves, produced an extraordinary clutter of sound. Programmes on this frontier of entertainment were often amateurish, sometimes vulgar, and soon tainted by advertising. Even so, radio proved immensely popular — by 1931, around one-third of Canadian households, and over one-half in urban Ontario, had a receiving set of some kind.

The efforts of American business and the Canadian state organized the new mass medium during the Depression. The maturing of American radio took place after 1927 when the National Broadcasting Company and the Columbia Broadcasting System, backed by Washington, fixed their stranglehold on programming. Within the next seven or eight years, the networks introduced a wide range of light entertainment, sponsored by brand name manufacturers — comedy like "Amos n' Andy," dance bands like "Fred Waring and his Pennsylvanians," whodunits such as the "Eno Crime Club" and drama such as "Lux Radio Theatre," soap operas like "Just Plain Bill," among many others. This fare, much of it presented for evening, family enjoyment, was enormously successful on both sides of the border. In his memoirs of the thirties, *The Winter Years*, James Gray recounts how radio-listening was a "passion" amongst prairie dwellers, whatever their means, for it broke the isolation of farm life and dispelled the gloom of Depression. Canadian business had just begun to respond to the ongoing craze by experimenting with sponsored and chain broadcasts. In fact, the Canadian Pacific Railway was willing to launch a private network. But the Depression intervened and the state acted. In 1928, Ottawa had finally set up a body, the Aird Commission, to investigate radio — its report recommending nationalization was partially implemented in 1932 with the creation of the Canadian Radio Broadcasting Commission, and four years later the Canadian Broadcasting Corporation. Canada acquired a dual system of local, private radio and national, public radio housed in a single regulatory framework. Immediately, the CBC embarked on an ambitious strategy of expansion and organization: new powerful stations were built, new broadcast regulations promulgated, network programming filled out, and services using private affiliates established for French and English Canada. By the end of the Depression, the percentage of Canadian households owning a radio had jumped to seventy-five, proof that radio was fast becoming a necessity of life.

The war marked the opening of the golden age of Canadian radio. The CBC had incorporated American offerings in its network programming and soon added its own brand of light entertainment, notably the farm serial drama "The Craigs" and the very popular variety show "The Happy Gang." During the war, the corporation captured a large share of the mass audience once addicted to American stations, so much so that in 1944 a second anglophone service (the Dominion network) was organized to supply more light entertainment. The CBC was thus able to offer commercial programmes like hockey broadcasts or "Fibber McGee and Molly" for the masses and sustaining programmes like Andrew Allan's "Stage" dramas or "Wednesday Night" for the more discerning. Private radio enjoyed an equal success: indeed, affiliates and independents grew in numbers and eventually broadcast power to the point where they threatened the planned CBC hegemony. Their local offerings of talent shows, newscasts, transcribed American programmes (like "Little Orphan Annie" or "Green Hornet"), current music, and the like were geared to the popular taste. So private radio watched with glee and greed as advertising revenues mounted steadily, up to $31,700,000 in 1954 for all radio stations. In that same year, a mere four percent of Canadian households lacked a radio. The prime listening time was undeniably the evening hours, when all stations offered versions of family entertainment. During the day, programming was less varied, except on CBC-owned stations, with music predominant, broken by soap operas in the afternoon and newscasts throughout the day. If moviegoing reigned supreme as the great family outing, then radio-listening ruled as the great home entertainment.

Neither the cinema nor radio seriously threatened the old print media. All made gains in popularity and profit. And books experienced a revolution of their own. By contrast with Western Europe, North America had earned a reputation as a book-poor continent. No more than half-a-million books were sold in any year in pre-World War II Canada, according to one estimate.[4] Publishers had at various times experimented with cheap reprint series, and during the 1920s book clubs had begun to reach a larger market through mail-order distribution, though neither technique dramatically changed the situation. What did was the paperback revolution born in Britain during the mid-1930s when Penguin Books began to merchandise cheap bestsellers. The Americans were not far behind, again finding a ready market for their books in Canada. In time, two Canadian entries appeared, Collins White Circle Books and Harlequin Books. By 1953, between twelve and fifteen million paperbacks were sold in Canada. The key to their success was a low price, mass distribution through drugstores and cigar stores, and above all the popular appeal of the offerings. Once more, the formula dominated, from science fiction and detective stories to historical romances and social melodrama. Still, if the biggest bestsellers remained, say, Mickey Spillane's violent exploits of Mike Hammer, by the early 1950s Penguin Books and various American publishers were striving for respectability with quality reprints and originals.

Magazines had also boomed. People were reading more, and the more included magazines. Those two very different anglophone weeklies, *Saturday Night* for the liberal-minded highbrow and the *Star*

Weekly for the ordinary Canadian, both reached a national readership. Another oldtimer, the Montreal Standard, merged with the Saturday edition of the Montreal Star in 1951 to become the Weekend Magazine, a newspaper supplement that would acquire carrier papers across the country. More novel were French Québec's weekend tabloids: first Le Petit Journal (1926), but soon followed by a host of others to create a distinct genre supplying news and gossip, sports and movie information, crime and social tragedy for the thousands. Particularly impressive, though was the Maclean-Hunter family of magazines: in 1950, Chatelaine claimed an average circulation of 374,000 and the amazing Maclean's Magazine 404,000. Maclean's, especially under the editorship of Ralph Allen, supplied an excellent variety of thoughtful and light articles, steadily more liberal, balanced with a bit of fiction, all for a middlebrow readership. It did face competition from the slightly sensational Liberty, an American offshoot Canadianized by Jack Kent Cooke in 1948 and turned into a monthly which sold over 400,000 copies by 1950. Rising fast on the horizon were the two "maple leaf" editions of Time and Reader's Digest, the latter with the fattest circulation (654,000) of any periodical.

Unfortunately, the swelling lists of subscribers made the consumer magazines more obese than healthy. Magazines had remained cheap, even as costs spiralled, to attract more readers, the publisher endeavouring to balance his losses on circulation with a higher advertising rate. That meant the food and drink industry, automobile companies, insurance corporations, and other normal clients had to be persuaded it was worthwhile to invest more money to reach the additional readers. Some publishers succeeded. For a time, Saturday Night was prosperous — in 1938 boasting the third largest volume of advertising lineage of any magazine in North America. In 1950, the four Maclean-Hunter enterprises (Maclean's itself, Chatelaine, Canadian Homes, and Mayfair) earned just over $4 million, more than half of the gross advertising revenues accruing to Canadian-owned leaders in the field. By comparison, Time Canada and Reader's Digest received $2,700,000, though more of this sum was profit because of the lower production costs of these satellites. But other publishers were less fortunate. In 1939, the old Canadian Magazine succumbed, so it claimed, to radio's competition for the advertiser's dollar. Almost ten years later, the new pictorial magazine, New World Illustrated, the Canadian imitation of Life, folded due to the disinterest of advertisers. In 1950, Liberty earned a paltry $700,000, insufficient to cover costs. Already, the pressure of costs had forced Saturday Night to begin a long period of experimentation with format and content to win more consumers and so more ad money. If the future was not yet bleak, publishers were haunted by the spectre of financial starvation.

The multimedia boom was a trifle upsetting to the daily press. Its stature as the "elder" medium, the fourth estate par excellence, was bound to suffer. In particular, publishers during the Depression worried about radio, a competitive advertising and news medium. As early as 1931, American statistics showed radio advertising had earned one-quarter of the sum hitherto expended on newspapers. Little wonder, then, that many dailies enthused over public radio, presumably funded by the people rather than commercials. Nor is it surprising that when the CBC announced in 1938 its commitment to commercial broadcasting, the daily press ranted and raved, a tantrum inspired by a sense of betrayal and some fear. The battle with radio, though, was fought over the issue of sponsored newscasts. The CRBC and later the CBC was allowed free use of "CP" copy as long as the network kept its newscasts pure, unsullied by commercial hucksterism. That agreement failed. Private stations took news from newspapers or other news agencies, and then sold newscast time to sponsors. Press efforts to ban such practices were always thwarted. Finally in 1941, "CP" surrendered, setting up a subsidiary (eventually called "Broadcast News") which sold bulletins to the CBC and private stations for commercial broadcast. Ironically, the surrender strengthened "CP's" position as the prime news source in the country, and enhanced the revenues of the cooperative. The last vestige of the press' news monopoly remained the Ottawa Press Gallery, which was closed to broadcasters until 1959. What had weakened the press war on radio was the increasing involvement of publishers in station ownership. The Southams and the Siftons could hardly be expected to favour a ban on sponsored newscasts that would cut their profits. Indeed in 1945, the pragmatic Roy Thomson urged his fellow publishers in the Canadian Daily Newspaper Association to buy into radio and, when the time came, television.

The daily press itself underwent few changes. Efforts to support radical dailies failed miserably: the Communist *Clarion* in the late 1930s, the equally Communist but very imaginative *Tribune* a decade later, and the "co-op" *Citizen* of Winnipeg also in the late 1940s proved unable to find sufficient revenue to survive. More spectacular was the sudden rush of tabloids which began in 1930 with the founding of *Montréal-Matin* (then called *L'Illustration*). After 1935, it was joined by the St. John *Citizen*, a newcomer, and the Vancouver *News-Herald*, once a nondescript morning paper. In Québec, three oldtimers converted to the tabloid format: *La Patrie* in the mid-1930s, the Montreal *Herald* near the end of the war, and *Le Canada* in the early 1950s. While their pictures, crime and scandal stories, local and sports focus all won lowbrow readers, none of the tabloids could generate enough money to prosper. By the late 1950s, just *Montréal-Matin*, a paper owned by the Union Nationale, survived. The problem was that a tabloid could only flourish with a huge readership, since advertisers thought its lowbrow readers were poor consumers. No Canadian tabloid was so fortunate.

The failure of the radicals and tabloids suggested how successful an enterprise the established newspaper had become. It covered its market like a blanket. Big city newspapers like the Halifax *Star* and *Mail* during the Depression, even more the Toronto *Star* or the Vancouver *Sun* well into the mid-century continued the practices of razzle-dazzle journalism which attracted lowbrow readers. Indeed, amongst the big stories of the era were the Lindbergh kidnapping and the Hauptmann trial, the birth and childhood of the Dionne quints, the Evelyn Dick murder case, and Marilyn Bell's famous swim of Lake Ontario — all sensational and entertaining. Still, after the Depression, most dailies assumed a more sober demeanor in keeping with their emphatic middlebrow approach to journalism. They supplied a profusion of trivia — all the greater because of the postwar expansion in the size of the newspaper — about the troubles of the world, the growth of the cities, and the happenings of the special worlds of fashion, sports, business, and the like. Competition lasted in some cities, especially furious in Toronto and Vancouver, but there was little fresh blood and weak newspapers continued to drop away. By 1945, such depletion had reduced the number of dailies to a low of eighty-seven. Although the conversion of weeklies into dailies in new cities brought the total up to ninety-four six years later, the result was merely an increase in the ranks of the single-newspaper centres. All of which enhanced the prosperity of the survivors. Profits had not been good during the Depression. After the war, though, newspapers benefited enormously from the good times. Between 1947 and 1957, the combined circulation of all dailies was actually greater than the number of households in Canada, signal proof of the hold the newspaper had upon the urban populace. In 1954, for example, the daily press secured $116 million in advertising revenue. Was it surprising that most publishers were satisfied with their lot?

What disturbed the peace of mind of publishers, radio interests, and moviemakers was the advent of television. Television was a much heralded medium — people had been talking about its arrival since the 1920s. Although the Hitler War slowed this arrival, thereafter American networks moved swiftly to launch commercial programming. Public pressure built up in Canada for the quick introduction of TV. In the early 1950s, Ottawa decided to finance a CBC controlled system that would reach out to all Canadians, an enormously expensive task. By 1960, the task was almost completed: Canada had forty-seven stations, nine belonging to the CBC and the rest to private interests. Soon after the CBC began broadcasting late in 1952, people and in particular, once again, the less affluent were eagerly purchasing sets. Three-quarters of Canadian households had television at the end of the decade.

The splurge of development did not bring stability. Unlike the earlier patterns of media expansion, television was subject to continuous shocks. In 1961, a new era arrived when the "second" stations opened in the big cities, eventually leading to the establishment of the privately-owned CTV network. Colour televison and colour broadcasting burst upon the scene after 1965. That was followed in the early 1970s by the introduction of Ultra-High Frequency broadcasting, the organization of Télé-Diffuseurs Associés (a private francophone network), the emergence of the Global network in southern Ontario, plus the appearance of TV Ontario an educational service. Since the mid-1960s, meanwhile, cablevision had spread very rapidly, first in major markets and later in the hinterland, winning subscribers with its promise of more channels and better reception. A decade later, almost all households had at least one television set, and over forty percent had a cable connection.

Even so, commercial television was for some entrepreneurs a license to print money.[5] National advertisers scrambled to use the airwaves to send their spiels to the unseen but huge television audience. The Davey Committee on the Mass Media, for instance, discovered that the biggest stations earned a before-tax profit on equity of 98.5 percent in 1964. The incredible profit margins began to slip in the 1970s as cablevision fostered audience fragmentation (better known as channel switching) and rising expenses raised costs. A new insecurity came to prevail amongst industry spokesmen, especially when they saw looming on the horizon such assorted innovations as a cable network, pay-TV, video tape recorders, and satellite broadcasting. Television, it seems, is locked into a permanent revolution.

Television proved an extraordinarily imitative, even parasitical, creature. It drew upon the practices (and the talent) of the rest of the multimedia to fill out its offerings. Much of the entertainment on television was modelled upon the afternoon and evening programming of commercial radio: soap operas, kid shows, sports broadcasts, quiz and variety shows, detective stories, comedies. No wonder early television was often called radio with pictures. But, in addition, television bought up all kinds of mouldy Hollywood films, later supplemented by newer and "made-for-TV" creations — the latter becoming the most recent version of the "B" movie. And, again following the Hollywood lead, television produced a host of stereotyped dramas, in serial form, about cowboys, cops and robbers, doctors, spies, and so on. Televised newscasts were a combination of radio bulletins, newspaper headlines, and the movie newsreels. Television's public affairs programming, which grew in significance from the early 1960s, emulated the radio talk and debate shows, newspaper interviews, or the magazine format. What television contributed to these formulas was impact. During the mid-sixties, "This Hour Has Seven Days," the sensational public affairs programme, used all manner of established techniques derived from print journalism with such flair and skill that it attained a hold upon the public mind no other magazine or newspaper had ever gained. Nearly everything on television became a spectacle, somehow more gripping, its immediate effect upon a mass audience at times frightening.

Much doom and gloom greeted the apparently inexorable march of television. The champions of print, radio, and movies feared their media were outclassed, if not outmoded. Television was a superlative, indeed unbeatable, mass medium, its competition bound to upset the older media. Besides, now that leisure time was reasonably fixed, television viewing was sure to cut into the hours people had spent with these other media. There was a brief decline in the paperback and comic book booms, though the former soon recovered its impetus. The increase in daily newspaper circulation slowed permanently, younger people in particular turning to television for the news. The old-fashioned consumer magazine was suddenly faced with the fate of the dinosaur. Giants like the *Canadian Home Journal*, *Liberty*, the *Family Herald*, even the *Star Weekly* — never mind pygmies like *La Revue Moderne* and *La Revue Populaire* — struggled manfully to no avail. The exodus of national advertising to televison simply made them uneconomic, a fact demonstrated by their disappearance in the next decade. Only *Time* Canada and *Reader's Digest* escaped relatively unscathed, as did their parents in the similar American debacle. Movie attendance slipped dramatically, though Hollywood rushed to compete with "3D" movies, wide screens, and assorted epics. By 1960, paid admissions were down over fifty percent from 1952. Going to the movies was no longer a common ritual of family life. Radio was almost totally eclipsed. Its entertainment and public affairs programming, personnel included, simply shifted to television. The American networks, after the super profits of television, stopped producing for radio. The CBC closed down the Dominion network in 1962. Few businesses have suffered such savage shocks as the communications industry in the 1950s. The memory of these years lingers on in the subconscious of the multimedia.

In time, however, the competition of television inspired a wave of innovation amongst the older media, indeed an eagerness to experiment with new ways to win consumer loyalty and advertising dollars. Radio struck back first. The popularity of the disc jockey on private radio stations pointed the way to recovery. This radio personality, a type born after 1945, gave a special tone through his patter and music to distinct segments of the day: the breakfast hours, the morning and lunch-time work period, the afternoon rest, the teenager's evening, and so on. By 1960, as well, private stations had already begun to specialize in particular brands of popular music, soon stereotyped as middle-of-the-road, rock, and country. The 'sixties witnessed the growth of so-called "Top 40" stations, CHUM Toronto perhaps the most notorious, which blared out regularly the ephemeral tunes on the hit parade for an audience of teenagers and young adults. More striking was the sudden rise of the "open" or "hot" line show, usually involving an aggressive announcer ready to exchange over the air opinions and insults with listeners who might telephone in. CBC radio, by contrast, turned to minority programming for housewives, music buffs, intellectuals, news addicts, New Canadians, culture-vultures, native peoples, and the like. And from the late 1960s, the FM boom added new diversity to the radio renaissance, with the promise of further changes such as all-news stations and a revival of the radio interview. These innovations worked. Listeners have acquired a special, sometimes a fanatical, loyalty to individual stations. Radio may have lost the evening audience, but it has remained the constant daytime companion of many, many Canadians.

The equally ravaged moviedom, once it gave up its foolish ambitions to outdo television, made a similar comeback. Like radio, Hollywood and its associates produced a wider diversity of offerings for many tastes, not just the mass taste. Particularly successful were Walt Disney's creations for the family, a host of beach-boy sagas and the like for teenagers, and the unending flood of pornography for the prurient. What might be called mainstream movies continued to follow the formulas of the past but with more attention to quality — of sorts. Sex and violence played their part, notably in movies like "Straw Dogs" and the rest of Sam Pekinpah's films. Criminals became human, indeed superhuman, in "Bonnie and Clyde" or the "Godfather" epics. Social drama was much complicated in "Who's Afraid of Virginia Woolf," "The Graduate," or "Midnight Cowboy." Even the western hero was parodied, notably by Paul Newman in "Butch Cassidy and the Sundance Kid" and "Judge Roy Bean." The "B" movie survived — witness most John Wayne thrillers or the more recent catastrophe series of movies — but it no longer seemed to dominate the screen. This catering to little audiences sparked the construction in shopping malls and downtown areas of multiple theatres with two, four, or more smallish rooms, each showing a different film. Overall, moviegoing had become a special occasion, though teenagers and the prurient were habitual consumers.

Much the same trends influenced the magazine press. General-interest publications survived, but only in the form of newspaper supplements like the *Canadian* and *Weekend/Perspectives*. The watchword for the rest of the press was specialization. The growth and prosperity of business periodicals in the 1950s and 1960s demonstrated that the specialized magazine had a bright future. The advertiser could be sure his message would reach the most likely buyers of his product at the lowest possible cost. That fact fact inspired the launching of city magazines, notably *Toronto Life* and the various "Calendar" periodicals. The latter series employed the newest technique of distribution, controlled circulation whereby a magazine is delivered free of charge to householders whose affluence suggests they will be excellent consumers. Another leader in this field was Comac Communications which in 1976 distributed *Homemaker's* and *Madame Au Foyer* to one and a half million households and *Quest*, primarily for men, to 700,000. That same year, *Mosaico* claimed to reach 80,000 Italian homes, the monthly representing a new force in periodical literature which catered to the prosperous New Canadians. In fact, the long-suffering *Saturday Night*, once virtually buried, arose again through new capital and aggressive promotion as English Canada's lucid journal of comment for the highbrow reader (boasting a paid circulation of around 90,000 by the end of 1976). Even so, none of these magazines seriously challenged the Maclean-Hunter empire which, after 1960, had finally extended into Québec with French editions of its circulation leaders. *Chatelaine* and *Miss Chatelaine* (amongst Canadian magazines) have together reigned over the women's market since the beginning of the 1960s. *Maclean's* had serious difficulties during that decade, when its sensationalist bias and assorted editorial troubles frightened away advertisers. But its mutation into Canada's newsmagazine in the mid-1970s produced a sudden revival of popularity, much enhanced after Ottawa killed *Time* Canada in 1976. Altogether, the validated circulation of consumer magazines rose from 5.7 million copies in 1961 to 16.2 million in 1975. Magazines regained their old status in the homes of the affluent as a common source of comment, information, and relaxation.

Even the newspaper press came cautiously to recognize the merit of innovation. After the mid-1950s, the big city dailies shed their penchant for social trivia, cut back on the coverage of world affairs, beefed up their surveillance of the local and national communities, and expanded their editorial and opinion offerings. Especially impressive were the early changes in *La Presse* and the Toronto *Star*, both of which awakened from a long slumber to gain a reputation for excellent, sometimes critical journalism. At one extreme, the highbrow newspapers, *Le Devoir* and the Toronto *Globe and Mail*, became famed purveyors of advocacy or opinionated reporting on political and economic affairs. At the other extreme, the tabloid revived with Pierre Péladeau's *Le Journal de Montréal* and *Le Journal de Québec* in the 1960s and the independent Toronto *Sun* in the early 1970s — this last a breezy dispenser of excellent photographs, a bit of cheesecake and much crime, lots of news trivia, and right-wing populism. Another new Toronto daily, *Corriere Canadese*, pointed to a further change, the rise of the ethnic daily as a force of some consequence in the mass press. Such innovations slowed the relative decline of the daily newspaper. That paper was unable to recover its pre-eminence of times past, however. Circulation increased steadily, though it did not keep pace with population growth. In fact, circulation figures actually dipped to 4.9 million in 1975 due to a general increase in the price of newspapers. Something more than a quarter of Canadian households did not take a daily.

What made these statistics all the more galling was the astonishing resurgence of the weekly press, for so long the forgotten rival of the big city daily. The weekly had taken its place within the ranks of the mass media during the 1960s. As a result of postwar immigration, ethnic newspapers grew steadily in numbers and circulation sufficient to win the attention of major advertisers. As a result of the postwar suburban boom, weeklies on the city fringe were infused with new life. Even the old country weeklies, aided by offset printing, had become more professional and more popular. The weekly supplied a pastiche of news about local or ethnic doings, from politics to weddings to sports, some comment and columns, and lots of retail ads, making it a superlative community medium. Overall, weekly circulation in the mid-1970s was probably around 8 or 9 million, evidence of the revival of parochialism amongst native as well as immigrant Canadians.

Beyond anything else, the advertising boom energized the astonishing mutation of radio, magazines, and newspapers. Since the war, net advertising expenditures have skyrocketed, from $122.5 million ($10 per person) in 1946 to over $1.7 billion ($76 per person) in 1974. Admittedly, all of this additional revenue did not end up in the hands of the media — indeed, since the mid-1950s, the market share of the media fell from well over three-quarters to around two-thirds, as businessmen employed direct mail and outdoor advertising in ever greater numbers. Still: between 1965 and 1975, ad monies for radio shot up 173%, for television 167%, for newspapers 139%, for consumer magazines 118%, and for class periodicals 40%. In 1975, the market shares were, respectively, 35.5% for newspapers (or $643 million), 13.5% for television ($245 million), 11.2% for radio ($203 million), 2.4% for consumer magazines ($43 million), and 2.3% for class periodicals ($42 million).[6] National advertising of liquor, cigarettes, cosmetics, soaps, automobiles, banks, insurance companies, travel, and so on have enriched television, consumer magazines, and dailies. Supermarkets and department stores, housing developers, business personnel departments, cinemas, furniture and clothing stores, a host of little buyers and sellers have further fattened the pocketbooks of big city publishers. Local retail advertising for a myriad of goods has bolstered the weekly press and private radio and television. Specialized firms have lavished ads for machinery and services upon business and farm periodicals. Bluntly put, the loosing of a golden stream of ad money excited the greed of so many media interests that their competition for wealth fostered an overall improvement in the performance of the communications industry.

Since 1960, the multimedia have emerged as the country's third mature system of communications. These multimedia differ substantially from their predecessors. Firstly, the multimedia are all engaged in mass communication. The lesser media of a bygone day have their successors in the mid-1970s, it is true, in the little magazines or the journals of combat, but their significance beyond the small coteries of readers is negligible. The country weeklies and the class press, once the key elements in the lesser media, have so organized their business, their contents, and their biases that they are definitely agents of mass communication. And the big three of dailies, radio, and television have vastly expanded the scope and sway of mass communication by comparison with their counterparts in early industrial Canada. Secondly, the multimedia constitute a diversified institution that serves a plural audience. At their heart lies television, the beast of burden, which furnishes information, comment, and entertainment suited to the mass taste. Worth noting, still, is the more specialized appeal of educational television on UHF channels and community service television via cable. The dailies remain, at least in metropolitan areas, the most complete source of news about life near and far. The buoyant magazines are approaching the status of a national print medium of reflection, some even bridging the language gap. The cinema and the book trade have become supermarkets of entertainment which offer a wide range of products to brighten everybody's day or evening. Private radio luxuriates as a daytime companion and a local service agency, public radio as the servant of large minorities. The ethnic and weekly press work to buttress the neighbourhood and the community once thought doomed in the mass society. Lastly, the multimedia cater, by and large, to the interests of the affluent majority. Obviously, some paperbacks and movies are geared to the supposedly vulgar tastes of Canada's social outsiders. Equally, television, because of the rating system, does offer programmes that please its heaviest users, namely the least affluent Canadians. But television, like all media heavily influenced by advertising, is geared to please the prime consumer. The newspapers (excepting perhaps· daily and Sunday tabloids), private and public radio, and in particular community weeklies and consumer or business magazines are even more concerned with satisfying the lucky citizenry. All considered, then, the present multimedia supply their clientele with an excellent service.

II

Part of the explanation for this excellence lies in the peculiar anatomy of the multimedia. A prominent feature of the recent history of the communications industry, again especially after 1960, has been a surge of media concentration which led to the formation of multimedia empires. By world standards, Canada seems to enjoy one of the highest rates of concentration amongst developed nations. The real pioneers of this concentration were a colourful crew of entrepreneurs: W. F. Herman, C. George McCullagh, Roy Thomson, Jack Kent Cooke, and the present John Bassett Sr. These men took immense pleasure in the game of acquisition: Bassett once admitted he was "a real pig," with an unbounded ambition to own more and more.[7] They showed no respect for convention and little for service, instead intent on profit and fun. Herman first played with a variety of Saskatchewan dailies, sold out to invade Ontario in 1918 by reorganizing the Windsor *Record* as the aggressive *Border Cities Star*, and briefly tried to revive a flagging Hamilton *Herald* in the early 1920s. McCullagh, "the Boy Millionaire," used the mining fortune of W. H. Wright in 1936 to buy first the Liberal *Globe* and soon after the Conservative *Mail and Empire*, then joining them in a marriage that took no account of tradition. Years later, in 1948, he purchased the Toronto *Telegram*, which together with the *Globe and Mail* engaged in a fierce struggle against the dominance of the *Star*. With equal flamboyance, though less viciousness, his protégé John Bassett continued the *Telegram*'s uphill struggle for twenty years until 1971, meanwhile buying into television and surburban weeklies. Beginning in northern Ontario during the Depression, Roy Thomson proved a voracious consumer first of radio stations and even more of small city weeklies, which he proceeded to convert into monopolistic dailies. During the 1950s, Jack Kent Cooke, Thomson's one-time associate, operated a string of consumer magazines including *Saturday Night*, *Liberty*, and the *Canadian Home Journal* in a fruitless attempt to challenge the Maclean-Hunter empire. Only Thomson really succeeded. The other entrepreneurs tried to assault the citadels of media power from its margins, an exercise in futility. Thomson, by contrast, challenged nobody. He built his own citadel, an empire that by 1975 included thirty-four dailies plus assorted weeklies and semi-weeklies. In fact, these holdings constituted only a minor portion of the world's largest media group, centred in England but extending throughout the British Isles into the United States as well as Africa and Asia.

Strange as it may seem, Roy Thomson found himself treated as a vulgar upstart in media circles during the 1940s and early 1950s. Prestige lay with the Southams, Siftons, and the Maclean-Hunter duo. Power did too. These aristocrats eventually moved, and with great success, to accumulate huge holdings. In 1953, the already sizeable Sifton chain of newspapers and radio stations split due to a clash between Clifford and Victor Sifton. Clifford, who acquired all but the Winnipeg *Free Press*, ran the Armadale company which by 1975 operated two daily newspapers (the Regina *Leader-Post* and Saskatoon *Star-Phoenix*), broadcasting stations in the west and Ontario, and a number of mixed businesses. More aggressive, Victor Sifton and his prime minister, R. S. Malone, parlayed the *Free Press* into a magnificent press empire (FP publications) through marriages with the equally energetic Max Bell, owner of his own western chain, R. Howard Webster of the *Globe and Mail,* and the McConnell family of the Montreal *Star*, picking up other properties along the way. During the early 1960s, Maclean-Hunter consolidated its grip on trade journals and expanded its magazine holdings into Québec; from the mid-1960s, the company descended upon broadcasting, cablevision, the book trade, and print distribution. But even this mighty conglomerate was dwarfed by the Southam empire, the true Leviathan of the communications industry. Relatively quiet since the early 1920s, this pioneer chain of newspapers suddenly acquired an insatiable hunger for press properties — by 1975, it operated seventeen dailies with a total circulation of nearly one million copies, a host of business publications, and assorted sundries. In 1976 Southam Press earned gross revenues of almost $300 million. That aside, its sizeable interest in Selkirk Holdings extended the Southam presence into radio, television, cablevision, and broadcast advertising, mostly in western Canada.

In addition, the enormous profits available in the communications industry attracted outside businessmen, indeed a trend that had its roots in the Laurier years. John W. McConnell, a sugar magnate, concluded an agreement (perhaps as early as 1917) whereby he would receive (which he did in 1938) the prosperous Montreal Star and its holdings on the death of Lord Atholstan. H. R. Robinson, a telephone promoter and multi-company director, acquired (during the course of the 1920s) the four St. John dailies, which he reduced to two, and later the city's private radio station. Robinson's holdings were absorbed in 1945 by the new R. C. Irving group which, over time, captured the other three anglophone dailies in the province and extended into television. These media properties, of course, were swamped by the multiplicity of businesses, estimated at around eighty, owned by the Irving group in the province by the mid-1970s. Also born in 1945, a new public company called Argus Corporation soon invested in radio by acquiring control of Standard Broadcasting (CFRB radio Toronto). After the 1950s, Argus used Standard to purchase CJAD radio in Montréal, expand into radio services and syndication, unsuccessfully battle for a Toronto television station, and finally secure in 1975 Bushnell Communications (CJOH-TV Ottawa plus cablevision interests and programming facilities). Argus' two billion dollar assets include as well Dominion stores, Massey Ferguson, Hollinger Mines, and Domtar. In 1975, Argus was almost swallowed up by another gigantic investment group, Paul Desmarais' Power Corporation. During the late 1960s and early 1970s, Desmarais had cut a swath through financial and corporate circles in Québec. One of his targets was media properties, and by 1975, through extraordinarily complicated lines of ownership, Desmarais controlled La Presse, four other francophone dailies, and assorted broadcasting facilities. Since Desmarais also has interests in Canada Steamship Lines, Imperial Life, Investors Group, and even Argus, his media empire is only one component of an awesome conglomerate.

There remain, of course, a variety of lesser kingdoms. Some are long-standing local monopolies, witness the Dennis family's two Halifax dailies or the Blackburn family's London Free Press and broadcasting outlets. More wide-ranging are such broadcasting groups as

CHUM Toronto with interests across the country, Moffat Communications on the prairies, or Western Broadcasting of Vancouver and elsewhere. Rising up are new entities like Pierre Péladeau's Québecor Inc., made up of daily and Sunday tabloids, plus many "pop" weeklies. Just as spectacular has been the post-1965 imperialism of the wealthy Toronto Star, which has gobbled up surburban weeklies (Metrospan), Comac Communications, and Harlequin Enterprises. Nor should the foreign interests be forgotten, such as McGraw-Hill Ryerson, so potent in book publishing, or the Famous Players and Odeon chains dominant in movie exhibition. Lastly, there flourishes that Crown corporation, the CBC, an anomalous body dependent more on tax money that advertising revenues yet moved by many of the same impulses as the private groups.

Few of the empires or lesser kingdoms are discrete entities. They interlock in a myriad of ways. Even CBC management has not been wholly isolated: Ernie Bushnell, for instance, went from private radio at the beginning of the 1930s into a long career as a CBC executive only to end up trying to fashion a television and cablevision empire at the close of the 1960s. Media owners, of course, share numerous contacts with the wider business community. More to the point, these owners meet and work together in their various organizations: the Canadian Daily Newspaper Publishers Association, the Canadian Association of Broadcasters, the Canadian Community Newspaper Association, or the Magazine Association of Canada and its rival Canadian Periodical Publishers' Association. All these organizations are fascinated by profits, leaving the issue of content and even ethics to other bodies. The raison d'être of the organizations remains to defend and enlarge the monies accruing to their particular segments of the communications industry. Indeed, the recent aggressive tactics of the CCNA have apparently paid off in attracting national advertisers to community weeklies. Beyond this, media owners have often joined together for some common aim. That news cooperative, "CP", is an excellent example of socialism at the top. But note also the Southam-FP alliance in Pacific-Press Ltd. to publish the Vancouver Province and Sun or the Southam-Toronto Star (Southstar) alliance to produce the Canadian. Where profit lies in cooperation, media owners are very friendly.

The masters of press, radio, and television do constitute a media elite. They are not a conspiracy against the public good, however. Indeed, their reign has contributed to a marked improvement in the performance of the media. The earlier generation of owners was better known for the neglect of their properties, and a lack of interest in public service: Pamphile DuTremblay and the Berthiaume family, for instance, almost gutted the money-making La Presse during the 1940s to support a grand style of living. The surge of media concentration merely demonstrated the communications industry was a business like any other, wherein bigness and growth were necessary to survive. The empires and kingdoms have enormous advantages because of their very size: economies of scale, a high credit rating, large pools of earned capital, and above all a capacity to adjust. Their resources in talent and money enable them to respond swiftly to market conditions. Hence their riches. The concentrated media do not yet have a stranglehold over the industry. There has remained room for newcomers to challenge vested interests on the frontiers of the industry: witness the recent tabloid revival or the appearance of "Calendar" magazines or the emergence of cablevision entities. Besides, the various empires have invested large sums to enhance their status or profits. For over forty years, the Southam chain financed a very respectable news service whose copy supplemented the international news of the ordinary wire agencies. Southam and FP might unite in Vancouver but fight in Winnipeg: Southam in 1975 lavishly supported the challenge of a revamped *Tribune* against the mighty *Free Press*. The Toronto *Star's* swelling possessions represent a new form of competition to a variety of other interests. No doubt the entrepreneurial element in the whole industry is small. But the stabilization of media markets was a function of the time of troubles during and after the Great War, not of recent media concentration.

The political clout of the media elite is also great, though hardly unlimited. The concentrated media did inherit the habit of direct intervention in editorial decisions from the publishers of the mass press. This habit was perpetuated into the 1950s by Jacob Nicol (*Le Soleil* and other francophone dailies). John McConnell (Montreal *Star*), George McCullagh (Toronto's *Globe and Mail*, later the *Telegram* as well), and Victor Sifton (Winnipeg *Free Press*). Nowadays, the social and economic assumptions of the media elite do find expression in the communications of their properties. Better yet, the owners can exercise a veto power over opinion, the ability to prevent the print or broadcasting media from consciously advancing a radical challenge to established ways. The New Brunswick dailies have received much abuse for their protection of sacred cows, namely other Irving enterprises, mostly because the newspapers have failed to investigate the assumed virtues of Irving's dominion. Desmarais' media have displayed a definite federalist bias, although that has not prevented *La Presse* and *Le Soleil* from supplying a reasoned coverage of the rise of separatism in their news columns. Indeed, whatever the sins of the concentrated media, they are more of omission than commission. The media elite has not evinced a concerted will to power, at least nothing comparable to the urges that drove the paper tyrants of bygone days. The Thomson newspapers have won a sad reputation for mediocre reporting — perhaps true, perhaps unfair — but hardly evidence of a dangerous partisanship. The Southam dailies, and now FP publications, are different newspapers with distinct traditions and perspectives. The assorted private broadcasting groups are not identified with any particular viewpoint. Overall, the concentrated media remain first instruments of profit, only second instruments of propaganda, whose economic strength has been a boon to mass communication and the affluent public.

Besides, a counterforce has emerged to challenge the authority of the owners and their managers. Running parallel to the surge of media concentration was the professionalization of the "working media," the journalists and artists who staff the communications industry. The roots of this professionalization reach back into the newsrooms of the 1930s. Then, the journalist was a poorly paid, almost powerless worker dependent upon the goodwill of the managing editor. A survey of pay scales during the late 1930s revealed a low starting wage, sometimes as little as $18 a week, slow and capricious increases, and a wide divergence of salary levels amongst men engaged in similar jobs (as much as $20 a week for one reporter and $70 a week for his compatriot on a rival newspaper). The reporter's situation was dismal, especially by comparison with the uniform pay scales and protection enjoyed by the unionized blue collar workers who produced the newspaper.

The exercise of managerial power at the Toronto *Star*, supposedly a pro-labour newspaper, demonstrated the impotence of the journalist. H. C. Hindmarsh, the *Star*'s dynamic manager, earned a reputation as a changeable tyrant, given both to benevolence and ruthlessness. He could be very sympathetic to the plight of the down-and-out, the drunk or the sick or the impoverished, willing to lighten their burdens or help their cure with additional funds. Yet he thought nothing of calling upon his excellent staff of reporters at any time, and of working them hard for days on end — without extra pay. He would not countenance compensation to reporters whose stories in the *Star* were syndicated — on other newspapers a welcome source of extra cash but at the *Star* merely additional revenue for the owners. More serious, Hindmarsh refused to satisfy the natural expectations of leading reporters for higher pay and some say in their work duties. "Prima donnas" he considered them, who deserved discipline. So even Frederick Griffin, the greatest *Star* reporter of them all, was humbled by being relegated to general reporting after some coup or other. Recalcitrance was punished by dismissal. The only way a journalist could escape such domination was to leave, something which a number of reporters did toward the end of 1945.

Unionization was the solution. The Depression-born American Newspaper Guild spread to Toronto in 1936, and soon after to Vancouver and Montréal. Managing editors were not especially sympathetic. The Toronto dailies, including the *Star*, broke the Guild in 1940 and 1941 when it strove for a collective agreement. By contrast, the Vancouver *Sun* did come to a settlement with the Guild over wages, severance pay, and overtime. That was the forerunner of a little flurry of contracts which coincided with a new upsurge of labour militancy in Canada at the end and just after the war. Le Syndicat des Journalistes was accredited as a bargaining agent for the staff of La Presse in 1944. Editorial workers secured an agreement in 1949 with management at the Ottawa Citizen. The same year the Guild finally won at the Star, the Telegram following suit in 1953, and the Globe and Mail finally in 1955. The Guild failed miserably in 1950, though, at "CP" as a result of managerial intransigence. Equal stubbornness by CBC management late in 1958 resulted in a bitter producers' strike in Québec, solved only in March of 1959 when the Corporation accepted the reality of the Association des réalisateurs. By this time, most managers had surrendered to the inevitable. The Guild, the Syndicat, and the Association of Canadian Television and Radio Artists were a powerful presence in newsrooms and studios across the nation. During the 1960s, CBC management proved particularly submissive to union pressures for higher wages and changed working conditions. Even where unions had been kept out, as in much of private radio, their example was felt. The result was a series of improvements in pay and security which raised the working media into the ranks of the affluent.

Of equal significance was the impact of the university. As early as the turn of the century, John Willison and other press reformers had looked to the university to turn out a host of new journalists who would improve the practices of newspaperdom. The reformers were a trifle early. Although a few dailies, notably Atkinson's Star, looked with favour upon university graduates, most editors were indifferent, selecting their reporters from wherever they could be found. Things changed after 1945. Some universities, aided by journalists like Wilfred Eggleston (an old Star reporter and a wartime censor), decided to follow the American lead by establishing schools of journalism. Carleton College (later University), the University of Western Ontario, and Ryerson Polytechnical Institute set up such schools during the 1940s and 1950s, remaining the leaders in the field of journalism education ever since. The liberal arts programmes of all universities, meanwhile, were producing more and more trained people in search of jobs. With the boom of the multimedia and the general rise of media wages, graduates turned in increasing numbers to jobs in the press and broadcasting. The graduate brought with him (and her, since many women found careers in the media) a new style and a new ethos. He expected affluence: not just good wages, security, reasonable hours, and promotions but freedom and even fame. He disdained the traditions of the old reporting and writing, less out of cynicism than a belief in his own superior knowledge of life. So he was more interested in opinionated or "soft" reporting, in questions of meaning and social responsibility, and in winning a by-line. There was a natural, often justified, and persistent resistance on the part of "oldsters," those trained on the job, to this new breed. And since many of the oldsters were in positions of authority, they could frustrate the ambitions of the newcomers. But, over time, this resistance was hopeless. By the mid-1970s, the university was the prime training ground for the working media.

In general, the staff now exercise a good deal of influence over the day-to-day communications of the multimedia. The size alone of some operations gives the individual much freedom. Because of their huge staffs and union pressure, big city newsrooms have moved toward a bureaucratized pattern of work in which tasks are identified and assigned, lines of authority regularized, power depersonalized. One result has been to convert newspeople in the press and broadcasting into "gatekeepers" whose sphere of authority, however limited, allows them to control the flow of information according to their own presumptions without much managerial supervision. The editorial staff of "CP" have a peculiar importance: theirs is the task of choosing, and choosing quickly, what will be sent to much of the news media from a mass of information available. The consequence is, of course, slanted copy, even though "CP" staffers clearly try to adhere to the dictum of objectivity.

Undeniably, the freedom allowed the new breed of journalists has much improved the quality of the media product. So observers have noted the growing sophistication of reportorial and editorial styles, a touch more perception in newspapers and magazines, a greater liveliness and variety in opinion. The Toronto *Globe and Mail*, for example, is a showcase for the best of this brand of journalism. At the same time, the new ways amongst reporters have resulted in some loss of the old virtues of objectivity and clarity, also true of the *Globe and Mail*. One reason for the success of the tabloids lies in the greater attention its reporters pay to reaching (rather than impressing) the reader with the facts. Even more important, the new ways have strengthened the traditional herd instinct among elements of the working media. Less encumbered by the rules of managers and owners, newspeople find inspiration from each other's ideas. In 1966, Don Jamieson, then a private broadcaster, sharply condemned "the intellectual inbreeding" that afflicted public affairs personnel in the CBC at Montréal and Toronto. Anthony Westell, a Toronto *Star* writer, repeated a wry comment from one reporter that in an election campaign members of the Ottawa Press Gallery "share everything but a salt lick." Sidney Freifeld, a one-time press officer with External, pinpointed an egregious instance of pack journalism: late in 1969, after Prime Minister Trudeau criticized the diplomatic service, editors and columnists across the country joined in a chorus of disparagement, one writer suggesting the service was engaged in lying and so much of its overseas establishment might easily be dispensed with.[8] Such rampant incest, of course, plagues virtually every profession.

The working media now constitute a rough kind of community at odds with the owners and managers of the industry. Inevitably, the thrust toward professionalism has moved to the second stage of a concern with ethics and a struggle for power. This became clear around the mid-1960s, albeit in a climate of public criticism of all institutions. Thus was born an assortment of professional associations, press clubs, even media conferences, wherein media people could mull over their grievances and express their yearnings. Partly in response, a new periodical entitled *Content* was successfully launched in the 1970s as the sometimes interesting, often jejune voice of the reform spirit in the news media. These musings have at times taken a more dangerous form among militants. In 1964, journalists at *La Presse* waged a fierce struggle with management over the control of editorial policy, and in 1966 a strike by Toronto's CBC producers over the cancellation of "This Hour Has Seven Days" was just barely avoided. Since then, there have been a variety of disputes, especially in the francophone media, over the respective rights of staff and managers. Indeed, Le Syndicat des Journalistes carried the battle a step further by pressuring the provincial government to intervene in the process of media concentration. One result of the agitation has been the proclamation by publishers and the like, sometimes in consultation with staff, of codes of ethics and practices that purport to define the roles of media personnel and the functions of the media in society. This has proceeded much further in francophone circles where journalists not only exercise the right to refuse unpleasant tasks but even, at times, to dissent from opinions management might wish voiced. So, in 1973, a branch of the Syndicat vetoed the publication in *Le Droit* of an anti-Parti Québécois column by Réal Caouette, on the grounds that the publication would contravene a newly signed collective agreement. Indeed, the failure of *Le Jour*, a separatist daily, in the summer of 1976 had much to do with the refusal of reporters to countenance any extension of managerial authority. Such evidences of reporter's power, of course, are still slight by European standards. The balance of power remains with management, emphatically so in the Maritime press. Nonetheless, the emerging sense of mission and solidarity amongst the working media promises a stormy future in labour-management relations and a slow erosion of managerial prerogatives. That, too, is likely to be a boon to the public, especially if the mood of professionalism spreads to some of the more benighted sections of the news media.

What prevents an irresponsible media, though, has always been the democratic imperative manifest in the logic of mass communication. The multimedia are subject to the discipline of the marketplace wherein the consumer's dollar is, at bottom, sovereign. The system has operated through newspaper and magazine circulations, box office and book sales, and the radio and television ratings. Since the Depression, these methods have been supplemented by market research carried out by media and advertising agencies, especially important nowadays in the case of controlled circulation magazines. In competitive markets, the system has been especially sensitive. Examples are legion in the history of the daily press. But even the CBC, partially isolated from the marketplace by tax monies, has evinced (whether out of a sense of pride or mission) a desire to compete with CTV and American channels in the fields of light entertainment and sports broadcasting. In fact, the steady growth of intermedia rivalry has brought the force of competition to bear upon even local newspaper and radio monopolies. The very recent revival of "ballyhoo" journalism, a new focus on crime, scandal, and exotica in all news media, is a direct response to the rediscovery that people like to be startled or thrilled by the news. Overall, the people get what is acceptable, not necessarily what they want. They exercise a veto via the withdrawal of their patronage, which compels media personnel constantly, and sometimes fearfully, to plumb the depths of public opinion. That restraint, in the end, is far more dependable than the continued forebearance of the media elite or the professional ideals of the working media.

III

The upshot of the constellation of forces always pushing and prodding the multimedia in different directions has been the production of a plethora of varied, often contradictory messages suited to a plural community and an open society. The democratic imperative, in particular, has worked to emphasize the cosmopolitan character of the Canadian system of communications. Few countries, nowadays, are free of the influences of outside media. The worldwide span of the American media is remarkable. In 1975, United Press International supplied half of the international news published in the world. Virtually all of the states of western Europe, and many of the nations of Asia and Africa, have felt the impact of the American style of entertainment. Even in Britain, where public broadcasting still looms large, television and more recently radio have undergone a process of Americanization. The enormous foreign presence in Canada's system, however, is singular amongst developed nations.

Canada's dependence upon the communications of other lands was natural in the first half or so of the nineteenth century. What made the Canadian experience special was the failure to escape such dependence. The advent of mass communications enhanced foreign influences, more properly swelled the volume of American messages entering the country. Some Canadian media were hopelessly crippled by American competition. After the failure of a few sporadic attempts to concoct an indigenous movie industry during and following the Great War, Hollywood effectively monopolized the Canadian cinema until the late 1940s — and the partially successful challenge then came from

European, not Canadian, moviemakers. A bit later, the book trade had succumbed, albeit in stages, to the successive waves of book clubs, paperbacks, and branch-plant publishers, mostly American in origin. Canadian magazines have always faced an uphill struggle against the overflow circulation of American publications, and since 1945 the enormous success of the "maple leaf" editions of *Reader's Digest* and the now defunct *Time* Canada. In 1974, American giants circulated a whopping 192 million copies, far surpassing the numbers of indigenous magazines, in Canada.

Beyond this, the Canadian media have commonly acted as the carriers of foreign messages. So book publishers long ago turned themselves into agents for the distribution of imports. "CP" was always dependent upon the "AP" international report, soon supplemented by Reuters' copy and recently by l'Agence France Presse. A large amount of the material in the dailies, notably after 1920, has been purchased from other, foreign news agencies and American syndicates supplying features and entertainment. Even public broadcasting has acted as a conduit for the mass entertainment of the Americans, less so the British and the French. And cablevision has really been a vehicle by which American television stations can enlarge their northern audiences at the expense of Canadian rivals.

Lastly, the multimedia have at times slavishly fashioned their offerings according to a foreign blueprint. During the golden age of radio, CBC news was modelled upon the BBC version; in recent years, television news has followed the American lead. The whole field of entertainment is littered with instances of imitation. Witness the recent "Jalna" fiasco on CBC television, an attempt to realize the kudos "The Forsyte Saga" gained for British television. Or the trickle of sexploitation films Canadian moviemakers have manufactured to fit some international standard of pornography. Better yet, the whole of rock radio which, when not broadcasting the American sound, purveys a blatant echo of that sound. By and large, the popular arts in Canada have remained stamped with a foreign imprint, either imports or facsimiles.[9] Altogether then, the multimedia have been both the victims and the associates of America's communications industry.

This notwithstanding, the indigenous element has waxed stronger over the years. Even the various advertising media have been partially Canadianized. So, during the Quiet Revolution of the early 1960s, the commercial messages directed toward French Canadians shed some of their American and Anglo-Canadian character to touch emotions close to the soul of Québec. The entertainment media have usually furnished some fare that was identifiably Canada. During the 1950s, Québec television won early fame because it supplied a gutsy, breezy, occasionally vulgar variety of comedy, music, and drama. In particular, the popular téléromans like "Les Plouffes" or later "Rue des Pignons" have perpetuated a bit of Québec's folk culture in the modern setting. By contrast, CBC's anglophone network has specialized in a wholesome fun, whether of the "Juliette" variety or the "Wayne and Schuster" comedy hours. But the news media are the most confident of these native voices. The recent rebirth of *Maclean's* as a national newsmagazine promises an addition to the slender ranks of the panCanadian news media. "CP", of course, has always been the pre-eminent agency of nationwide communications because it supplies clients across the land with a rich variety of Canadian news. Consequently, the agency is a much more effective progenitor of consensus than, say, the CBC whose French and English networks were thoroughly segregated after 1938. Not to discount the significance of the talks department on CBC radio years ago or the public affairs department later on CBC television, both of which produced a brand of commentary on life that was emphatically Canadian. René Lévesque's "Point de Mire" in the late 1950s, "This Hour Has Seven Days" in the mid-1960s, CTV's "Inquiry" in the early 1970s, or CBC radio's "As It Happens" in the mid-1970s were all startling instances of the innovative, often brilliant style of media controversy not uncommon in Canada. Where the indigenous element has remained predominant, then, is in the focus upon the public ways of the country — its politicians, courts, trade unions, business affairs, livelihoods, mores, and worries.

The hybrid nature of the communications system is linked to the economics of the industry. The small size of the Canadian market makes difficult the profitable manufacture of a multitude of unique messages. The proximity to the huge market of the United States has meant a natural overflow of American media and messages. The excellence of the Hollywood movie, for instance, made idiotic the continued efforts to compete by any native entrepreneurs — at least until government funds were available. The very cheapness of the American product, whether in the form of international news or syndicated features or radio transcriptions or telefilms, proved an irresistible attraction to a media eager for new material. So live television drama on CBC's English network was in large part killed during the late 1950s by the purchase of American serials priced at a mere $2000 per half-hour episode. Even the Québec network was soon seduced by the low price and high appeal of dubbed American comedy and of French movies. The savings that resulted and the ad revenues that accrued, though, helped to fund the remaining species of light and highbrow entertainment as well as the boom in public affairs programming during the 1960s. The Canadian multimedia have simply lacked the resources to compete with the cheap excellence of the popular arts manufactured elsewhere.

At bottom, however, the status quo has reflected consumer satisfaction. Canadians have consistently demonstrated their preference for the trivia and the fantasy, the news and culture of outsiders. As far back as the late nineteenth century, the people's dailies pioneered by publishing numerous American features, from sermons to comedy, which obviously caught the fancy of the masses. CBC radio's success during the 1940s was due, in part, to its transmission of American entertainment which appealed to all sorts of listeners. A Gallup Poll in 1975 showed that 57% of all Canadians rated American televison programmes superior to British and Canadian.[10] Even so, the public has displayed a loyalty to its native voices. Newspapers have never been seriously threatened by foreign competition. The consumer magazines suffered in the 1950s and 1960s because of a loss of advertising revenue, more than a loss of readers. The birth of network hockey broadcasts in the early 1930s first weaned Canadian listeners away from American stations. French-Canadian television immediately became a tribal medium, enormously popular with the Québécois. CBC radio has an equally devoted, if smaller, audience across English Canada. The contradiction is more apparent than real. The hybrid communications system has offered a consumer's paradise of delights suitable for a diversity of tastes and interests. No wonder the system has survived nationalist obloquy.

The accommodation of foreign and indigenous communications perpetuates a peculiar kind of duality whose roots go back into the nineteenth century. The popular arts in Canada have always been foreign, never alien. The much-feared "Americanization of Canada" was a fact in 1900, at least everywhere outside Québec, as Samuel Moffet gleefully pointed out.[11] The triumph of the multimedia not only strengthened American influences in English Canada, but extended their sphere into French Canada. Indeed, this very Americanization fostered a common social ethos which acts as a national bond. More and more people in every generation have shared the slang, the heroes and villains, the myths, the values, the ambitions of an American design sufficient to maintain a sense of community amongst Canadians. The popular arts have been a counterweight to the sectional and ethnic differences within Canada, thus allowing these to flourish without so far shattering the political fabric of the country. Americanization, from this perspective, is a necessary balance to that Canadian mosaic served by the indigenous communications. Their focus upon public ways nourished an allegiance to Canada, or better yet fostered a pyramid of loyalties to place, province, the "two solitudes," and the nation-state. In particular, the news media in each province have buttressed a series of distinct political cultures and forwarded assorted parochial identities. Equally effective, at least up to the 1970s, the commentary of these media endeavoured to renew the committment of every generation to a federal structure that worked to harmonize parochial ambitions and national goals. The apparent dichotomy of the popular arts and the public ways, of course, is a fiction of analysis rather than a reality of life. Neither are purely foreign nor native: there exists a "Canadian" style of entertainment as well as an "American" flood of news. More important, the two types of messages interweave in an incredibly complicated fashion to mould such diverse notions as personal morality, the rule of law, or the concept of social justice. What the identification of the dichotomy displays, though, is one vital foundation of that Canadian characteristic, "unity in diversity.".

This knowledge, furthermore, helps to explain the causes of the perpetual identity crisis that has bothered anglophone intellectuals since the Great War. Nationalists have been frustrated by the task of defining a Canada so very American. Undeniably, the enormous volume of American communications has posed a threat to Canadian independence. The resulting fascination with the political trivia of the United States in the years just after World War II fostered a dangerous acceptance of America's will to power. These were the years, after all, when Canada emerged briefly as the little Cold Warrior, ready to echo the anti-communist hysteria of the American empire. These were also the years when roughly one-fifth of Canadians expressed in polls a willingness to join the United States. But that suicidal urge was an aberration. The American presence did not prevent the emergence of a new revulsion against the United States amongst the literati of English Canada during the mid-1960s. Familiarity, at least in the Canadian experience, breeds both emulation and contempt. One of the most consistent themes in the literature of Anglo-Canadian nationalism is the assumption of Canada's superiority, usually a moral superiority. Canada has been, so it would seem, a better America, boasting the virtues of affluence and order, liberty without license, internationalism but not imperialism. However illusory such notions, however unsatisfactory to the professional nationalist, their re-occurrence suggests they remain the basis of a sense of national identity amongst the wider public.

At the core of this definition of the Canadian identity lies the ideal of affluence — and no wonder, given the influences working on the public mind. The impact of the advertising media has been particularly striking. Especially since the end of World War II, the huckster intruded with impunity into Canadian homes. Better yet, he used the sophisticated techniques derived from motivational research to tailor his spiels to play upon the emotions. Greed, envy, fear, ambition, self-consciousness, all have been grist for his mill. The adman manipulated the desire to stand out as well as conform, the language of snobbery and of equality, the yearning for security and the spirit of adventure. Successively, he beat down resistance to such one-time novelties as personal deodorants, convenience foods, or stylish men's fashions. Soft drinks he linked to youth, sex appeal has sold cars, buying insurance was tied to protecting the family, and on and on. Advertising was behind many of the emerging mores of the affluent society: the smoking habit that made cigarettes a symbol of adulthood; the mechanization of the home that relieved wives of the drudgery of housework; the incredible cult of beauty with its clean-shaven men, sanitized women, well-scrubbed teeth, and sweet-smelling armpits. Whatever the individual products the advertiser might boost, advertising merchandised a distinct life-style which revolved around the ideal of consumption. Advertising overcame the habit of thrift by emphasizing the virtues of indulgence. The purchase of goods and services became the route to personal happiness and social status. New festivals of consumption were created out of old holidays, such as Christmas and Easter, or simply fashioned out of hallowed traditions, such as Mother's and Father's Days. Masses of anonymous people were joined in ephemeral "consumption communities,"[12] defined by the common use of identical goods. Even the family became pre-eminently a unit of consumption, with mother the chief buyer and father the happy provider. By no means all people were seduced by the messages of the advertiser, in the 1920s or the 1970s. Advertising joined a complex of disciplines, some like religion the critic of needless consumption, that pushed people in different directions. But sufficient people were motivated by advertising to engender a spending spree that has made Canada, like the United States, a land of conspicuous consumption and enormous waste.

The entertainment media enhanced the pleasures of affluence. The entertainer satisfied a huge clientele with a panoply of distinct (though not exclusive) tastes. Never before had the highbrow enjoyed a richer fare of the good things in life. From the beginning, CBC radio was determined to feed the Canadian soul with the best of the world's music and the inspirations of Canadian playwrights. An important by-product was the strengthening of a native culture industry with small but dedicated coteries of fans across the country. If CBC television has not quite matched the achievements of radio, still by the 1960s the highbrow could choose from a selection of avant-garde films, quality paperbacks, or FM stations to satisfy his habit. Every advance in mass communication has benefited the devotees of high culture.

So, too, the lowbrow found his needs well-served. During the 1920s, and 1930s, Macfadden Publications released a gush of adventure tales, romances, and true stories. Over time, these were supplemented by pulp fiction and comic books, crime thrillers by Mickey Spillane and his ilk, unnumbered Harlequin romances about love's anguish and exotic places, and eventually a surfeit of pornography. Movies also contributed their share: especially after the mid-1950s, the dream factories turned out hundreds of teenage pictures and "skin" flicks. Perhaps most charming, though, were the soap operas of radio and later television, which were supposed to comfort the housewife. The quality of all this lowbrow entertainment might be slight, but the range of topics was wide — from brutal violence and nauseating sex to sentimentalized romance and rigid morality. Altogether, these items offered relief and escape, in particular for people outside the mainstream or oppressed by society's demands.

The greatest amount of entertainment, of course, was aimed at the middlebrow consumer. In fact, nearly everyone has found something to his taste in the wealth of bestsellers, popular music, "B" movies and epics, children's fare, serial dramas, variety and family shows, quiz programmes, and sports broadcasts. These, the true popular arts have stolen themes and subjects from the highbrow and lowbrow genres: witness the movie vulgarizations of Shakespeare and the Bible or television's penchant for violence. This brand of entertainment has become the prime source of the mythology of the affluent. The ethnic folklore of a past age, the Christian and British and even French-Canadian traditions of the people have been subsumed in the standardized fantasy of the multimedia. Western sagas turned the American prairies into the historical heartland of North American civilization; gangster movies and the like have perpetuated fears of the unsafe streets, a continuation of the Victorian belief in the evil city; horror stories and weird exotica have fashioned a dread of the unknown, the irrational, the supernatural. Likewise, the popular arts have spewed forth a series of heroes for every generation — movie, sports, television, and singing stars, some of whom like Babe Ruth or Clark Gable or Marilyn Monroe have achieved immortality. Beyond all else, these arts have fixed in the popular mind the image of the rugged individual who battles fate and circumstance to achieve some ambition. This fantasy and diversion, then, defined the stereotypes, the hopes and fears, the heroes and villains of modern living for Canadians irrespective of age, class, and language.

The evolution of the news media was also marked by a shift toward diversity. Slowly, these media came to play a more independent role in public life, a role befitting their pride, prosperity, and power. The most obvious change occurred in their relationship with the parties. Broadcasting never fell under the partisan spell. Admittedly, the rise of radio during the 1930s fashioned a new weapon of considerable potency in the struggle for votes. "Bible Bill" Aberhart used radio to transform his fundamentalist congregation into a Social Credit movement that swept to power in the Alberta election of 1935. His achievement was all the more startling because he lacked either a party machine or a farm organization to topple the government. The newly organized Union Nationale employed radio in 1935 and 1936 to castigate the corruption and incompetence of the Taschereau government, part of a campaign that ended forty years of Liberal rule in Québec. Even the Bennett Conservatives endeavoured to stem the tide of defeat with a few scurrilous broadcasts, the so-called "Mr. Sage" incident.[13] Soon after, though, the CBC moved to neutralize radio as a partisan force. The famous "White Paper," finalized in 1944, provided for free time political broadcasts by all parliamentary parties during and between elections, and allowed the purchase of additional time on private stations within each province or for local campaigns. These dicta nicely fitted the mood of private radio which had no interest in forwarding a partisan cause that might alienate listeners. In fact, the CBC did manage to enrage the federal Conservatives during and after the war by its bias toward the Liberal government. Even so, the notion that broadcasting must be a forum of partisan opinions was firmly entrenched in the political culture.

By contrast, the party press, a once honoured institution in this political culture, suffered a lingering death after the Depression. Newspapers found neither profit not plaudits in serving a party, so they were free to indulge their principles or their fancies. True, partisan bias did not disappear from the pages of the press: in national politics at least, newspapers commonly favoured either the Liberal or Conservative parties at election time on the front pages and in editorials. But the old consistency had gone, especially in the provincial arenas where third parties and particular issues played a prominent role. Sometimes, personal relations were a factor: so, after 1936, George McCullagh (Toronto *Globe and Mail*) backed his flamboyant buddy, Mitch Hepburn; just as, after 1946, J. W. McConnell (Montreal *Star*) cheered on his new-found friend, Maurice Duplessis. Indeed, most dailies in Québec, whatever their language or supposed loyalties, swung behind the Duplessis regime, partly because le chef favoured publishers with government largesse but even more because he delivered on the promise of social peace plus economic development. Similarly in Alberta, the Edmonton *Journal* (less so the Calgary *Herald*) which had once waged a furious war against Aberhart actually proclaimed the virtues of Manning's conservative style of good government in the late 1940s. Not so in Saskatchewan, where the reality of a CCF government made the Liberal *Leader-Post* and *Star-Phoenix* shrill champions of free enterprise against a red tide. Nor in Ontario: during the federal election campaign of 1949, the *Telegram* and the *Star* resurrected the practices of a bygone day by blatantly slanting their news reports, all part of a grudge fight between the two afternoon dailies. (This campaign ended with the first edition of the *Star* carrying the infamous headline KEEP CANADA BRITISH / DESTROY DREW'S HOUDE / GOD SAVE THE KING, dropped in later editions.) As a rule, monopoly newspapers tried especially hard to avoid irritating any readers or advertisers with an undue bias. When the Dennis family bought out the opposition in Halifax in 1949, the resulting *Chronicle-Herald* and *Mail-Star* foreswore all partisan loyalties. More serious, the leading dailies proved ready to break away from their erstwhile mentors in times of crisis. During the 1963 election campaign, for example, such Conservative stalwarts as the *Globe and Mail*, the *Telegram*, the Montreal *Gazette*, and the Calgary *Herald* savaged John Diefenbaker and his government. In the 1974 election, the Toronto *Star* caused a stir by joining its two rivals in a common assault on the Trudeau government. Newspapers, it seemed, could change their politics with almost as much ease as their format. In fact, a complex of factors (local conditions, the business situation, ideological perspectives) determined the politics of newspapers, now that the partisan imperative was so weak.

A new, uneasy relationship between politicians and the news media took shape after the mid-1950s. Altogether, the mass media succumbed to a strange schizophrenia, at once the tool of the political leader and the voice of popular grievances. The news media still gave the assorted thoughts and activities of politicians a top billing. In particular, the party leader found television a marvellous instrument for reaching into the nation's living rooms. The televised leadership convention, special broadcasts, election advertising, and routine interviews publicized the personality and the opinions of the leader far beyond any means known to his predecessors. First Louis St. Laurent, later John Diefenbaker, and recently Pierre Trudeau attained the stature of mass leaders with a personal following amongst the electorate. In all, a fuehrer principle has come to influence the course of politics. At the same time, though, the journalist assumed the role of the public's watchdog, eager to find fault or favour irrespective of party. That dated from the trauma of the Pipeline debate of 1956 when the bitter exchanges amongst warring parliamentarians infected the copy of the Press Gallery. Before long, the Press Gallery became something of an unofficial opposition to the parties. So the Gallery first boomed and later damned Diefenbaker, first welcomed and later ridiculed Pearson, first embraced but soon jilted Trudeau. (Not all reporters, of course: the Liberal Bruce Hutchison and the Conservative Peter Dempson, for instance, continued into the 1960s the older habit of partisan reporting.) The Gallery's waywardness was just the most obvious manifestation of a new mood that was turning elements of the news media into an adversary of partisan authorities. The press decided it had a dispensation to hunt out scandal, damn incompetence, suggest alternatives, or call for new leadership. Thus, after the 1972 provincial election, the Toronto *Globe and Mail* constituted for a time a vigorous but nonpartisan critic of the apparently invulnerable Davis government in Ontario. Perhaps more significant, the press has articulated the loud provincialist challenges to Ottawa (whatever the ruling party) that in the past two decades have seriously complicated the task of national government. Little wonder politicians, so often the butt of media criticism, have responded with denunciations of the irresponsible press. Not only has parliament's prestige suffered, but also the old-style national party which depended upon partisan fealty to ensure cohesion and consensus. Even the once magnificent Liberal party has collapsed into a ramshackle collection of disorganized zealots and disgruntled souls that no longer comprehends the ambitions of the nation. The mass leader and the news media are fast turning politics into their story of marriage and divorce.

Running parallel was the dissolution of that intellectual freeze which had afflicted the commentary of so many opinion-makers in the 1920s. True enough, the right-wing stance of the press was perpetuated well beyond the war. Throughout, much of the daily press extolled the virtues of free enterprise and warned against the seductions of radicalism. In the Depression, newspapers often played the role of the booster — sure prosperity was just around the corner if people would only have faith. The public debt, the Montreal *Star* believed, was the number one problem besetting the land, a problem radicals would only make worse.[14] During and after the war, when good times did return, the same press took seriously the need to banish the socialist spectre that haunted Canada's golden future. So, in the election campaign of 1945, the Halifax *Chronicle* was much exercised by "the gilded ball and chain of national socialism" (6 June) offered electors by "the rabble of radicals trailing noisily in Mr. Caldwell's wake" (11 June), namely the Co-operative Commonwealth Federation. Many editorialists, infected by anti-red hysteria, continued to distrust government intervention and enterprise (including the CBC), especially as long as the CCF seemed a menace and labour unions were militant. At the beginning of a new decade, *Maclean's* (15 November, 1950, 2) solemnly proclaimed the duty to make war on communism in whatever its guise. The press campaigns deflected the vague public desire for a social reconstruction and stymied CCF efforts to win favour in central Canada. The fever of the reaction only began to wane by the early 1950s, when the struggle to save free enterprise seemed won.

Even so, the news media had slowly come to accept the legitimacy of dissent. The roots of this acceptance reached back to the tradition of eccentricity which runs through the annals of journalism. During the Depression, however dominant the restraint of conformity, some newspapers flirted with a weird variety of crotchets. The Vancouver *Sun* wondered about the merits of technocracy, *L'Action Catholique* endorsed a brand of corporatism, the Ottawa *Citizen* thought Social Credit a panacea for economic ills. Early in 1939, George McCullagh used his *Globe and Mail* and radio broadcasts to launch a "Leadership" campaign, which amounted to a call for cheap government and business rule. Joe Atkinson's *Star* displayed so much sympathy for the workingman, the CCF, and the Soviet experiment that it acquired such nicknames as "the Red Star" and "the Daily Pravda."[15] But most eccentric was that habitual crusader, *Le Devoir*, which warred against the many enemies of "la survivance" Catholic style. In particular, the newspaper won much notoriety for its lonely criticism of the sins of the postwar Duplessis regime. Purportedly, that earned the paper sufficient enmity to prevent most corporations from placing an ad in its columns.

The CBC pioneered the new acceptance of dissent, though, by its commitment to controversial broadcasting. This, the corporation thought, was part of its responsibility to educate the public. Even in the 1930s, the corporation mounted round table discussions to express a variety of viewpoints on topical issues. During the war, in league with voluntary associations, it launched the famous "forums" in French and English for rural and urban listeners. These forums dealt with such sensitive questions as social equity and social security, wages and prices, labour and management, international affairs, and so on. After the war, labour and business spokesmen were invited to debate issues on a broad range of economic subjects. Assorted broadcasts focussed upon marriage, child-rearing, and mental health. Equally provocative were educational programmes that delved into life and its meaning: so, in 1951, three series on astronomy, psychiatry, and philosophy which placed in doubt religious truths won the CBC a torrent of abuse. Indeed, the practice of controversial broadcasting, however tame, raised the ire of red-baiters, anxious businessmen, and assorted moralists. If the CBC sometimes backed down, its proud support of the talks department did ensure a forum for dissent and debate.

After 1960, much of the news media embraced dissent. Controversy was suddenly a hot item. People wanted to be jolted. Private radio's open-line broadcasts lent themselves to crude, vigorous commentaries upon marriage and morality, children and adolescents, jobs and work. Although occasionally liberal in tone (witness Larry Solway's "Speak Your Mind" on CHUM Toronto in the 1960s), more often the shows voiced a right-wing populism that decried, say, teenage smoking or socialized medicine. Pat Burns earned CKGM Montreal a censure from the Canadian Radio-Television Commission in 1968 because of his offensive, supposedly anti-French, approach to issues. Television's public affairs programming, while more sophisticated, also slipped into sensationalism by offering up weird interviews, assorted confrontations, or spectacular exposés. But it did so usually on behalf of a liberal or left-wing criticism of existing attitudes and institutions. So "Close-Up," "Inquiry," and later "This Hour Has Seven Days" turned a spotlight on, for instance, old age and poverty as well as the Stephen Truscott case and the Ku Klux Klan in an effort to excite or entertain viewers. Meanwhile, newspapers had opened their columns to different, striking opinions. The Edmonton *Journal* started "The Journal for Dissent" opposite its editorial page, the Toronto *Telegram* offered an assortment of clashing columnists, the Toronto *Star* gave "The People" a voice by publishing their abbreviated and emotional letters. Early on, *La Presse* took up the cudgels for the Quiet Revolution with such fervour that even provincial Liberals were disturbed. In a similar vein, the

Toronto *Star* had become by the late 1960s the foremost champion in the press of the "new nationalism" of English Canada. In general, the metropolitan newspapers and radio and television stations had shouldered again the age-old responsibility for criticizing their communities — censoring the authorities, questioning the virtues of development or expressways, or exposing business frauds. The news media, then, were the boosters of that confused mixture of criticism, dissent, and utopianism which led the 1960s down strange pathways in an effort to engineer the good society.

The chief legacy of this sometimes wild era of experimentation was the conversion of the news media into a surprisingly faithful mirror of the public scene. The media still, by and large, distrust a thoroughgoing radicalism. Neither separatism in French Canada nor social democracy in English Canada have received much direct support in print or on the air. Also, the news media still display a faith in the justice of the institutions (from the marketplace to the political party) that distribute power in modern Canada. The campaign the press has waged in the 1970s against inflation suggests that the priority remains the defence of affluence rather than the reform of society. But leading dailies and magazines, the television networks and CBC radio, especially the "CP" news agency have come to reflect the range of opinions in the country. What has been called the "fairness doctrine," the need for balance in news and comment, has much influenced broadcasting and even affected print journalism. So media surveillance extends far beyond the domain of the establishment or the trivia of life to the anger of labour, the plight of the poor, the agitation of reformers, the discoveries of science, and the new if ephemeral manners of the public. Assorted groups of intransigents, from the Right to Life to the Dene Nation, are able to get their messages through the media's sieve. Overall, media scrutiny seems to favour criticism more than celebration. This, on balance, has worked more to the advantage of novelty (whether the advance of the interventionist state or the new morality or women's lib), than to the old-fashioned (whether the growth ethic or private enterprise or marriage). For granted the power of communications, the news media have widened the definition of respectability and lessened the force of orthodoxy. The news media, nowadays, are just as often the vehicles of conflict and change as consensus and stability.

Different pressures have moulded that other voice of diversity, the oft-neglected ethnic media. The massive influx of European immigrants in the first postwar decade soon inspired a general renaissance of the foreign-language press, eager to preserve the memories of the homeland. By 1960, Marika Robert discovered ninety-three ethnic newspapers, published in twenty-nine languages and read by an estimated one and a half million people. The majority of these papers espoused an ethnocentric and anti-communist line which made them fervent supporters of the Cold War and Canadian democracy (when not squabbling over past ethnic feuds). If this pattern continued, still the more successful amongst the ethnic media have responded to the wiles of affluence by adjusting to the Canadian milieu. So there have emerged a special news and feature service ("The Canadian Scene"), two German-language chains (the *Torontoer Zeitung* group and Courier Press), commercial radio stations (CFMB Montreal and CHIN Toronto), an Italian daily full of the normal Canadian fare *(Corriere Canadese)*. Slowly, the ethnic media have acquired a new justification, the advance of multiculturalism — which can mean the preservation of the old heritage, the reform of Canadian ways, the pursuit of a new definition of Canadian citizenship. In short, the ethnic media have remained a third force, neither francophone nor anglophone, which gives substance to the ideal of a Canadian mosaic.

None of the media, of course, act alone. Advertising, entertainment, and news flow together to fashion images for the public. The arrival of the liberated woman has been heralded not only by news reports and editorial comments, but by advertisements that incorporate feminist jargon and television dramas or comedies that star versatile heroines. The recent impression of a plague of violence owes as much to television's fantasy as the front page's reality. All of which suggests an apparent paradox about the plethora of images so produced. From one perspective, the consumer can choose from a wealth of moods (ranging from optimism to pessimism), stereotypes (the "sick" society or the "progressive" land), and emotions (satisfaction or alienation) to interpret life. But the images offered the consumer are not infinite. Most are bounded by the fact of affluence. For the multimedia have become, above all, the voices of affluence. Their influence has supplemented, revamped, corroded, and sometimes replaced older attitudes. In particular, that Victorian ethos so prominent before the Hitler War has suffered, if not quite dissipated. Admittedly, such old-fashioned catchwords as "property rights," "home sweet home," "law and order," and "the virtues of work" survive in a changed form, sometimes in the adman's jargon. But the Victorian legacy serves more as a storehouse of criticism from which the red tory or the vulgar conservative may select weapons to do battle with modern sins. What stands forth now, for instance, are human rights, the nuclear family, social justice, and consumerism. The multimedia, then, have attained a sway over the popular consciousness and conscience, that no other institution can boast.

IV

The recognition of the power of communications has often inspired a good deal of anxiety. A poll conducted for the Davey Committee revealed that nine out of ten Canadians believed the media exercised some influence on thought and life-style. The same poll showed about two-thirds of the respondents favoured a form of control over the content of the multimedia. This finding points to an important social reflex which has conditioned the history of the media for roughly a century. From at least the 1870s, the rise of mass communication has provoked a defensive reaction from assorted interests and institutions that felt their authority or ideals threatened by its power. Churchmen, politicians, businessmen, women's groups, labour leaders, reformers of all stripes, literary and academic intellectuals, even journalists have joined in a series of campaigns to protect society against some noxious effect. The reaction has been justified by a peculiar alliance of forces: puritanism and traditionalism, snobbery and Babbittry, patriotism and profit, radicalism and conservatism. Sometimes the critics have urged private actions — say a boycott of an offending newspaper. But, much more important, the critics have demanded the state take steps to stem the menace the media pose to the common good. Herein lies the source of a resurgent authoritarianism which, especially in recent years, has extended the authority of the state over the multimedia and their messages.

The first concern was the saving of Victorian Canada and its chosen technique was a moral protectionism. By the late nineteenth century, anxious commentators found in circulation too much pernicious literature — irreligious or seditious works, penny dreadfuls and dime novels, and cheap, illustrated magazines. While dangerous especially to the unformed minds of the young and the feeble intellects of the poor, this pernicious literature supposedly posed a threat to the moral health of everyone. "The moral circulatory system is poisoned, the very springs of orderly living are corrupted at the fountain, and the social fabric of Christian society is placed in jeopardy," cried the Toronto Mail (15 October, 1881). Common law provided some protection against obscene publications, and in 1892 a clause in the Criminal Code made the sale of such works an indictable offense. Sabbatarian legislation largely prevented the appearance of what seemed a despicable species of American immorality, the Sunday newspaper. But the first line of defence for proper Canada was the tariff. Moralists assumed that pernicious literature came largely from other lands, especially the United States. By Confederation, a section of the Customs Act, strengthened in 1879, prohibited the entry of indecent and treasonous matter. Over time, the Customs department built up what amounted to a Canadian index of forbidden works. As late as 1949, the department tried to protect Canadian readers from the influences of Leon Trotsky's Chapters From My Diary, D. H. Lawrence's Lady Chatterley's Lover, James Joyce's Ulysses, Herman Rukin's Eugenics and Sex Harmony, "The Awful Disclosures of Maria Monk," plus a wide assortment of obscure trash. The tariff was, it seemed, a good deal more effective in keeping out foreign books than foreign manufactures.

After the Great War, a new form of moral protectionism, movie censorship, won acceptance across Canada. The very popularity of moviegoing amongst families made Hollywood's vulgarity a threat to public morals, again particularly to children. Free trade in "diseased films," noted an anonymous censor, was just as inimical to the community as free trade in "diseased meat."[16] The Catholic spokesmen of French Canada were especially upset by what they regarded as the insidious immorality fostered by American movies. The upshot was the strengthening of censorship laws in all provinces to preserve decency. A survey of censorship in 1940 demonstrated that the puritans were certainly aggressive. Eight years before, they had banned 101 full-length features; though because of the activities of the Catholic Legion of Decency and the Hays Office, Hollywood had cleaned up its product. Still, censors were forced to cut out scenes with too much passion or lust, excessive violence and horror, or suspicious language. Nor did they take kindly to movies that questioned religion or any orthodoxy. Apparently in Ontario, pictures of riots or strikes were usually removed from newsreels, and throughout the country scenes like the May Day parade in Moscow were taboo. Little wonder a movie like "The Grapes of Wrath" was edited to ensure it did not cast doubt upon the virtues of democracy. Indeed, so vigilant were the boards that in time O. J. Silverthorne, long chief censor of Ontario, was moved to declare, "Canada is the most over-censored country in the world and ridiculous in the eyes of cultured nations."[17]

That statement, however, showed that the legitimacy of censorship was under attack. The changing mores of postwar Canada moved the country further and further away from the Victorian certitudes of the past. During the 1950s and 1960s, liberal-minded souls especially in the culture industry launched a series of challenges to the structure of moral protection. It gave way. The cry of artistic freedom and the gathering forces of the new morality sent the puritans into retreat. Slowly, the state leashed the moral instincts of the custom's officials, watered down the legal definition of obscenity, and limited the zeal of the censor. Bookstores could purchase virtually whatever foreign works they thought might sell. Moviehouses could show much that might seem obscene by adopting a classified system which warned prospective patrons of the moral quality of the picture being shown. The happy principle of artistic freedom, of course, had allowed — in fact, justified — a new era of license. Along with the so-called quality movie or book of a dubious character came a much larger quantity of pornographic and sadistic fare. The police and the courts could not halt the spread of this moral pollution. Actually, it was all part of the flourishing of a lowbrow life-style with its own conventions displayed in such places as Toronto's Yonge street "Strip," indeed in big cities across North America.

More lasting was the impact of a second wave of reaction which mobilized the country to save the Canadian nation. This spawned a cultural protectionism designed to hold back the forces of Americanization. The spread of American culture, of course, had long been a cause for alarm. But it suddenly acquired great strength in the 1920s. That decade of contrasts witnessed the birth or expansion of a number of voluntary associations devoted to Canada first, which sponsored a new efflorescence of francophone and anglophone nationalisms. In this climate of opinion, public attention was soon focussed upon the expanding American communications empire, manifested by the galloping circulation of its magazines, the dominance of Hollywood, and the popularity of American radio. Under the nationalist banner, Canada boosters, publishers and puritans, and highbrows struck out against the empire. The magazine publishers linked patriotism to profit by demanding a duty on American periodicals, something Bennett's government agreed to in 1931. The highbrows leading the Canadian Radio League forwarded their aim of quality, noncommercial broadcasting by converting the same government to the wisdom of public radio. Although stymied by Hollywood's monopoly, the nationalists' case underlay the decision of the King government to set up the National Film Board in 1939, as a medium whereby Canadians could interpret their own experience. The achievements of this reaction were, to say the least, imperfect. The Bennett tax on American magazines was repealed by the King government in 1936. The CBC was forced by listeners and costs to carry American programmes and commercial messages. The NFB produced a wealth of documentaries which, however important, did not disturb the foreign hold over the mass cinema. The nationalist crusade had lost its way somewhere in the Depression and during the war.

Prosperity brought a rebirth of cultural protectionism, this time sponsored by royal commissions. In 1951, the seminal Massey Report recommended that the government adopt a cultural strategy designed to sponsor excellence and Canadianism. Some years later, the Fowler Report pressed for more Canadian televison and the O'Leary Report urged protection for Canadian magazines. By the mid-1960s, another "new nationalism" had captured the fancy of assorted writers and academics, mostly in Toronto and environs, though their influence spread far and wide. What was necessary to slay the American dragon, so it seemed, was a vigorous policy of Canadianization to patriate the communications industry. If hesitant to seriously challenge the advance of America's economic imperialism, the Liberals and their bureaucrats soon proved eager to secure cultural sovereignty. The campaign, though never sufficient to satisfy nationalists, certainly upset American interests, at times the communications industry, and occasionally the ordinary Canadian. It all began with the birth of the Canada Council in 1957 to fund excellence, or at least literary, artistic, and academic endeavours. The newly-formed Board of Broadcast Governors announced in 1959 future "Canadian content" regulations to govern television programming, though a generous definition (that declared the World Series and presidential speeches Canadian) made the effort a trifle ludicrous. Canadian ownership of the magazine and newspaper press was ensured in 1965 by a change in the income tax law which prevented any taxpayer from claiming a deduction for advertising placed in a foreign-owned publication. The CDNPA, in vain, denounced this interference with freedom of the press. By contrast, Reader's Digest and Time Canada won an exemption, largely because Washington brought pressure to bear on the Pearson government. The Canadian Film Development Corporation was set up in 1967 to sponsor an infant movie industry, which fed lustily off the public teat but produced little that was Canadian or successful. Later, voluntary agreements were negotiated with the foreign-owned cinema chains to display a certain number of Canadian-made films each year. A new broadcasting overseer, the Canadian Radio-Television Commission launched in 1968 under the command of the nationalist Pierre Juneau, immediately set to to "save" the country: it forced American interests to divest themselves of cable and television holdings, tightened up the "Canadian content" rules, and soon extended a similar regulation to radio. Thereafter, the CRTC worked to Canadianize cable, if only by forcing the companies to delete random American commercials in their offerings to the public. That provoked cries of piracy and a threat of a border TV war from outraged American stations. Meanwhile, the Secretary of State, and the provincial authorities in Québec and Ontario, employed a series of subsidies to save a native book trade. In 1976, the Ottawa government finally killed Time Canada and turned on American television stations directly, by extending the scope of the discriminatory income tax law. So it goes. In all, the Canadian state has elaborated a formidable system of cultural protectionism, impressive proof of the impact of nationalism and the elitism of Ottawa.

The nationalist crusade, likewise a reawakening puritanism, have now merged with the third wave of reaction to save the Canadian democracy. Here, the enemy is an irresponsible media and the answer a gospel of social protection. Again, the concern over the performance of the "fourth estate" was long-standing. Had not John Beverley Robinson warned against the dangers of a seditious press? After the fall of the tory order, the courts were assigned the task of protecting the individual against an abusive newspaper. A thicket of libel laws forced a modicum of responsibility upon the otherwise uncaring journalists. In the Great War, the government took up the emergency power to censor the news media, if necessary to ban a seditious publication. By and large, the daily press voluntarily submitted to the state's regulations in this time of crisis. However irritating certain capricious decisions, the ordinary powers of the courts and the wartime authority of the government were deemed necessary to the public good.

Things changed. The experience of the Great War seemingly demonstrated the awesome power of propaganda. The communist upheaval sparked a struggle for men's minds. The rise of the multimedia inevitably disturbed the earlier accord between government and the press. The arrival of radio required that the state grant frequencies to radio stations to avoid chaos. The initial disinterest in radio programming soon gave way before the public's complaints over hucksterism and propaganda on the air. In 1928, the government deprived the International Bible Students (the future Jehovah's Witnesses) of their four stations, apparently because their proselytizing zeal and anti-Catholic opinions antagonized the Catholic church. Some years later, the CRBC prohibited the broadcast of the speeches of Judge Rutherford, the Witness leader. The Commission also moved against commercials, in particular patent medicine and stock promotion advertising, notorious for their wild claims. At the end of the 1930s, the CBC set down regulations that placed religious programmes under the authority of the established churches and assured such broadcasting would emphasize Christian harmony. This paralleled the "White Paper" on political broadcasting which ensured only respectable parties would voice their opinions on the CBC network. First George McCullagh's "Leadership" campaign and later the anti-conscriptionist propaganda of the Ligue pour la défense du Canada suffered the results.

Meanwhile, the print media found their practices under scrutiny. In the mid-1920s, parliamentarians denounced "CP," then the recipient of a subsidy, as a dangerous monopoly. Tommy Church, the maverick Conservative, carried the campaign into the 1930s by sponsoring a bill to force the press' disclosure of its financial masters. In 1937, the Duplessis government in Québec passed the infamous Padlock Act which gave the attorney-general sweeping powers to crush any publication tainted with communism. The same year, the Aberhart government introduced the even more contentious Alberta Press Act. Aberhart thought the daily press was the instrument of finance capitalism, so bound to undo his Social Credit regime. The act, in effect, promised to close down any newspaper in the province failing to publish official statements or indulging in too much criticism of the government. Canadian publishers moved quickly to defeat this "gag law," though eventually they were beholden to the courts for its unlamented burial.

Soon after, publishers and broadcasters were forced to submit to the controls of a wartime government. Indeed, the multimedia, and especially the CBC, became the ideological arm of the state in its effort to boost morale and the war effort. It is not surprising that publishers began to wonder about the wisdom of a constitutional guarantee for the free press and broadcasters to lash out against the CBC's authority. In fact, the authoritarian impulse waned during the happy years of postwar prosperity. The anti-socialist rhetoric of press and business buttressed a climate of opinion hostile to big government. Even the CBC's supervision of private radio suffered.

There were signs of trouble ahead, though. Labour and the left justly railed at the daily press over its self-evident bias against their cause. Before long, the ideas of a new heresy began to seep into Canada. During the 1940s, an American and a British commission both investigating press performance articulated what was soon termed the "social responsibility" theory of communications.[18] Underlying the doctrine was the presumption that the condition of the media determined the fate of democracy. The theory asserted the news media in particular, and by implication the whole of the communications industry, must become a public utility dispensing truth. Apparently, truth meant accurate news, a total picture of life, a wide range of opinions, and avoidance of sensationalism. Advocates hoped the multimedia would voluntarily submit to this regimen; if not, then the state had the duty to promote responsibility.

After 1960, a storm of criticism swept over the communications industry. Left and right, politicians and puritans, nationalists and reformers, business and labour found sufficient cause to condemn the arrogance, the profits, the irresponsibility of the multimedia. Charges of yellow journalism were hurled at the news media, of perversion at television entertainment, of deceit at advertising. No doubt the advent and impact of television provoked some of this ire. Television's apparent hold on the minds of young and old alike frightened people. But more important was the critical perspective of the decade which questioned the legitimacy of all institutions. The multimedia was especially vulnerable because the images they manufactured were bound to anger some interest. Inevitably, the state attempted to realize the vague ideal of social responsibility. In 1970, the report of the Davey Committee lambasted media concentration and media performance, urging government to induce diversity and competition in the industry. Then, the Combines Branch launched an assault upon the Irving empire in New Brunswick. The always zealous CRTC blocked the combination of cable and television holdings by a single company, sponsored the Global network to bring more diversity to Canadian televison, and even planned "FM" offerings to ensure balanced programming. Lately, Ontario's LaMarsh Commission has led the revived legions of decency against violence in print and on the screen. The embattled media responded with the cry that freedom of communications was imperilled. Public displeasure, though, inspired promises of good behaviour, the organization of press councils to hear complaints, even the setting aside of nonviolent "family hours" on television. Nothing the multimedia said or did could quiet the storm of criticism. For the aim of the agitation remains less a responsible press or a decent television than a humbled media. The organized community was and is moving against an institution whose overweening power seems to threaten the fabric of democratic society.

The ebb and flow of these successive reactions has left a definite mark on the whole process of communications. In general, the state has worked to impose upon the media whatever values might be current amongst the enlightened public. Much of the past activities of the state, of course, were limited to prevention. Book banning and movie censorship tried to stop the spread of evil. Likewise, the libel laws, the controls on misleading advertising, and the ownership regulations performed a similar, negative function. In recent decades, however, the state came to play a more positive role. The establishment of the CBC was the first striking evidence of the state's readiness to realize an elitist definition of the proper communications. So far, the continued respect for the principles of a free press and private enterprise have restrained the state's ambitions. Besides, the marketplace has fashioned a multimedia that still appears to many people a democratic institution. So the poll of the Davey Committee revealed most people were generally satisfied with the service. Unfortunately, the now current social responsibility theory justifies an easy recourse to authoritarian measures. Ironically, a person otherwise happy with his television entertainment or newspaper can always find something, perhaps too many ads or too much sex and violence or too little good news, that deserves correction. Worse yet, the public acceptance of protectionism has allowed an aggressive state to arrogate the powers necessary to achieve certain esteemed goals. So, in 1975, the Ottawa government employed a special definition of nationality in the process of destroying *Time* Canada, a ruling that extended the state's purview over what appears in the magazine press.[19] Already, bureaucracy has eaten deeply into the autonomy of broadcasting on behalf of the shibboleth of cultural sovereignty. The only obstacle to the arrogance of the CRTC lies in the stirrings of a provincial challenge, notably from Québec and Saskatchewan, to Ottawa's authority over cablevision. Even so, the multimedia are faced with the spectre of big government, of an ever-widening sphere of official controls.

V

Much of the animus toward the multimedia has had its origins in ignorance. Throughout the twentieth century, newspapers, movies, and television have been blamed for everything from a moral breakdown to a business recession. Such charges reflect a widespread assumption about the omnipotence of mass communication. Not even the multimedia, however, can lay claim to divine powers. There is little doubt, of course, about the public's addiction to these media. Radio supplies background noise in many homes throughout the day; newspaper readers spend roughly a half hour perusing their favourite daily;

viewing television can consume upwards of twenty-four hours a week, and more in the case of children. Something around two-thirds of the population read during their leisure time, a group which comprehends all ages and all classes. About a quarter of Canadians, mostly teenagers and young adults, are regular moviegoers. An uncounted number of people spend time with class and ethnic journals, community weeklies, and magazines. The individual pattern of use can differ widely. The consumer selects the media and the messages that suit his preoccupations, his bias. Information, excitement, relaxation, companionship, these are only a few among a long list of possible gratifications. What he learns depends upon what he already believes. So a conservative might well discover in the news traces of a creeping socialism that would seem to a radical signs of a business-government alliance. Communications are more likely to confirm an existing opinion than to change the opinion. That accounts for the consistent failure of media campaigns to alter the loyalties of the partisan at election time. There have always been limits to the impact of mass communications, especially the immediate impact, upon the public mind.

The import of the multimedia lies in society's dependence upon the process of mass communication for images of life. People live in a common ideological environment which is sustained by a continuous flow of information. Nothing momentous, not politics nor the economy nor leisure, can function properly without this flow. No wonder the citizen feels bereft when a strike deprives him of his regular newspaper. His ability to understand events in the city or the nation is sadly restricted. Out of such dependence grow the variety of specific effects of mass communication: the multimedia reinforce established opinions, amplify the strength of some, set the agenda of public concerns, and thereby mobilize people in the political arena or the marketplace. The front page of a newspaper and the national news of television play a central role in the routine of politics by identifying issues and personalities, a fact which explains the interest the party leader takes in the lead items on the news. The advertising media alert people to a product or service, indeed sell people on the idea of purchase, an effect that accounts for the phenomenal success of such food franchise operations as McDonald's Hamburgers and the like. Going a step further, media recognition and repetition casts a garb of legitimacy about any novelty, whether a person or an event or an idea. So, during the early 1940s, the focus upon social security gave that onetime heresy a general credence. By the same token, the attention the media devoted to the drug culture of the 1960s worried older generations because it threatened to justify that culture. In the end, the process of mass communication supports the cohesion of the affluent society. The multimedia are leading agents of social control because they legitimate the dominant institutional and cultural patterns of authority. Unlike premodern lands wherein an individual normally followed in the footsteps of his forefathers, for late twentieth-century Canada the media directly or indirectly furnish the individual with his guides to behaviour. In particular, the multimedia popularize a uniform way of life and a consensus of values, both predicated on affluence. Since communications are much more flexible, indeed ephemeral, than the dictates of tradition, the affluent society compensates for its apparent instability by a capacity to undergo rapid social and economic change without a major upset. Even a superficial survey of the incredible variety of technological innovations, from the car to the computer, that have altered people's lives since the Great War should illustrate this adaptability. A reign of fashion has finally succeeded the supremacy of tradition.

The reign of fashion, though, has not given birth to that nightmare of the radical and the conservative alike, the so-called mass society. Typically, critics have used this term to suggest a society characterized by mediocrity, alienation, homogeneity, conformity, passivity and on and on, leading apparently to de facto totalitarianism.[20] Admittedly, the autonomy of the other leading social institutions has declined in recent decades. Harold Innis was rightly worried about the future of the ideal of scholarship that had justified the university as an ivory tower. The multimedia portrayed the university as an intellectual factory that manufactured a trained work force and a crew of social experts, a conception that underlay the state-financed multiversity of the 1960s. More generally, the multimedia usurped the moral authority previously shared by the church and the school, undermined the critical perspective of trade unions, and conditioned the child-rearing practices hitherto the preserve of the family. But these institutions have not been blighted. Far from it. While the corrosive effect of communications met with resistance, witness the church's long battle against the immorality of the mass press and cinema, eventually there has been an accommodation with the multimedia, often leading to an adjustment of values and practices. So, in Canada as elsewhere, religious broadcasting has been something of an ecumenical force in the Christian brotherhood. Since the 1960s, the academic has used the daily press and television to convey his arguments to a wider audience, suggesting perhaps the birth of a mild form of the meritocracy? The recent boom in professional and labour militancy is linked to the news media's recognition of the virtues of solidarity in the marketplace. Better yet, the family has remained the central social institution (if such there is), but now as a unit of consumption which employs the multimedia to enjoy the wares of abundance. Whereas the isolation of the various social institutions is a thing of the past, their power and significance clearly remains.

Much the same situation prevails in the region of popular culture. The devastation of folkways and the like by the multimedia may be tragic. The countryside stopped boasting a distinctive ethos soon after the 1930s when radio, in particular, broke the isolation of the past. Social classes lost definition in the postwar era because the dream of affluence purveyed by the multimedia was substantiated. The traditional values of a Catholic Québec finally gave way to the modern values of the North American media after the mid-1950s. But the sharing of a common ethos has hardly ended the pluralism of Canadian life. The expansion of the multimedia after 1945 was paralleled by a recreational revolution which sent people off to the ski slopes, trekking or skidooing through field and forest, into basements to pursue assorted hobbies, off to the lake or sea to sun and swim, and through the gates of innumerable sports stadiums, museums, galleries, and tourist palaces. Likewise, the advance of television occurred at the very moment when English Canada finally experienced that longed-for literary and artistic awakening oft-proclaimed by previous generations of intellectuals. Perhaps most striking, the multimedia have encouraged the persistence of many publics across the land. A complex of national voluntary associations (i.e. the Canadian Clubs and the Canadian League, the League of Nations Society, the Round Table Movement, the National Council of Education) spread out over Canada during that very decade, the 1920s, when the multimedia began their march. Some of these, their successors, and the farm organizations as well found in radio during the 1930s and 1940s a very useful instrument for the dissemination of ideas. Québec's acceptance of the mores of affluence after the mid-century was linked to an upsurge of nationalism, especially evident in the big city press and Radio-Canada, which threatens to end the nation-state. Elsewhere in Canada, multiculturalism has come to the fore, and seems likely to wax ever more significant with the growing prominence of the ethnic press. Overall, the emergence of issues like capital punishment and abortion, separatism, native rights, economic nationalism, and so on demonstrate that the wellsprings of bitter contention are as full as ever.

All of which raises the perennial "national question," the survival of Canadian unity and the winning of Canadian independence. Here, the effects of the multimedia have been decidedly mixed. Not that they are the culprits, but only contributors to the national distemper. For the survival of the nation-state relied, in part, upon the persistence of certain traditions: the British connection, partisan loyalties, and Ottawa's pre-eminence. First to go was the definition of Canada as a British Dominion in an Imperial family of nations, a notion Carlton McNaught found widespread in the prewar anglophone press and H. F. Angus and company found amongst its readers. The North Americanism the multimedia purveyed after 1940 justified Canada's inclusion in the imperial orbit of the United States. More serious, perhaps, was the decline of the partisan loyalties which had made the major parties instruments of national unity. The news emphasis upon individual leaders, at the provincial as well as the national level, has fragmented the political system. Beyond that, the lifting of the partisan restraint upon parochialism animated an assortment of provincial and regional grievances against the authority of Ottawa. And the focus upon Washington was at the expense of Ottawa, cultivating amongst some Canadians the impression that the prosperity of their provinces depended upon events transpiring in a foreign capital. Admittedly, the news media have often, consciously, boosted Canada. That is especially true of the CBC: time and time again, it has dedicated some programme to a celebration of the Canadian experience. Since the late 1960s, leading newspapers have accorded the ideal of a bicultural Canada a sympathetic hearing, hopeful that the implementation of the ideal would foster a greater French-Canadian commitment to the country. Some news outlets, such as the Toronto *Star* or *Maclean's*, have sponsored a panCanadian nationalism grounded in a rejection of American domination. A few, *Le Devoir* for example, have articulated a new conception of federalism resting upon a radical decentralization of authority. To little avail, though. All in all, the multimedia have encouraged a climate of opinion hostile to the old Dominion and Confederation, without generating any widely accepted alternative opinion that might support some new national order. Therein lies one reason for the present-day fragility of the nation-state.

No-one can really predict the future of the multimedia. Too many factors may affect its destiny. The waning of the advertising boom would deprive the print and electronic media of their lifeblood, indeed of the incentive to serve a plural audience. An upsurge of authoritarianism could well undermine the democratic imperative and transform the multimedia into an elitist institution. A radical decentralizaton of political power, or the collapse of the nation-state, would of course disrupt the whole system of communications. In particular, technological innovation is bound to alter the structure, perhaps the import as well, of the multimedia. Video recorders and pay TV will likely endanger the fortunes of the cinema and the television station. Communications satellites will enhance the cultural invasion by messages from foreign lands. Mass information utilities of computer banks and receiver networks will constitute a much more potent national news medium than hitherto available. The widespread use of a two-way cablevision system would dramatically alter the process of mass communication itself, hitherto really a monologue but for open-line radio. Perhaps, then, the admitted four out of ten Canadians who talk back to their radio or television sets could better express their momentary frustrations. Clearly, the much-touted dream of public access to the media would acquire substance. What all this means, of course, is that like any other institution the only certainty about the future of the multimedia is change.

Notes

[1] Noted in A. Sangster, "On the Air," *Canadian Forum* (March 1953), p. 281.

[2] M. Rosenfeld, "How TV is changing your life," *Maclean's Magazine* (1 December, 1954), p. 87.

[3] J. S. Woodsworth, *My Neighbor*, Social History of Canada reprint (Toronto: University of Toronto Press, 1972), pp. 91-93.

[4] M. Denison, "Big Little Books," *Maclean's Magazine* (15 December, 1945), p. 43.

[5] That phrase, of course, has entered the folklore of television. Roy Thomson coined it in 1957 when talking about his Scottish television station. Since then, the phrase has inspired entrepreneurs, worried governments, infuriated radicals and nationalists, and intrigued writers. Rarely has a phrase so quickly and so completely become a cliché for everyone.

[6] See The Financial Post Report on Media, *Financial Post* (1 May, 1976).

[7] Quoted in M. Zwelling, "The Paper That Couldn't," in Dick Macdonald, editor, *The Media Game* (Montreal: Content Publishing Limited, 1972), p. 116.

[8] Respectively, D. Jamieson, *The Troubled Air* (Fredericton: Brunswick Press, 1966), p. 163; A. Westell, "Reporting the Nation's Business," in G. S. Adam, editor, *Journalism, Communication and the Law* (Scarborough: Prentice-Hall, 1976), p. 63; S. A. Freifeld, "The Press Officer and External Affairs," *International Journal*, 31 (Spring 1976), pp. 261-262.

[9] The "popular arts" refers to the music, the literature, the comic books, the motion pictures, the television films, even the advertising dispensed by the multimedia for the general pleasure of humanity. See B. Rosenberg and D. M. White, *Mass Culture. The Popular Arts in America* (New York: The Free Press, 1957.)

[10] 10% preferred British, 19% Canadian, and 14% made no judgement. In Québec, only 46% preferred American, compared to 6% for British, 34% for Canadian, and 14% "Don't Know." By age, two-thirds of those respondents under thirty preferred American offerings. Cited in the Toronto *Star*, (27 December, 1975), B3.

[11] S. E. Moffet, *The Americanization of Canada*, Social History of Canada reprint (Toronto: University of Toronto Press, 1972), (original 1907).

[12] See D. J. Boorstin, *The Americans. The Democratic Experience* (New York: Random House, 1973), pp. 89-164.

[13] The "Mr. Sage" broadcasts were a series of dramatized political discussions, paid for by the Conservative party though its sponsorship was never clearly announced, which criticized Liberal policies and even besmirched Mackenzie King.

[14] For instance, on 1 August, 1938 the paper carried the slogan on its editorial page "A NATION'S HEALTH IS A NATION'S WEALTH;" on 2 August its cartoon linked individualism with intelligence; on 3 August it praised Finance Minister Dunning as a man of sanity standing against "financial will-'o-the-wisps"; and on 4 August the editorial entitled "THE MONEY YOU OWE" warned readers action was necessary now to relieve the debt burden crushing "the economic and social machinery of Canada."

[15] See William L. Archer, "Joe Atkinson's Toronto Star. The Genius of Crooked Lane," Montréal, a right-wing pamphlet apparently written around 1946.

[16] A Censor, "The Censorship of Moving Pictures," *Dalhousie Review*, 1 (April 1921), p. 41.

[17] Cited in J. R. Kidd, "Films," in J. Irving, editor, *Mass Media in Canada* (Toronto: Ryerson, 1962), p. 74.

[18] See F. S. Siebert, T. Peterson, W. Schramm, *Four Theories of the Press* (Urbana: University of Illinois Press, 1973), pp. 73-103.

[19] The government refused to exempt Time Canada from the income tax law unless eighty percent of its matter was essentially Canadian. See Geoffrey Stevens' columns on 3, 5, and 10 December, 1975 in the *Globe and Mail* and "Ottawa Marks Time" on 13 December, 1975 in the same paper.

[20] Of course, the alarm over the mass society has found a wide variety of expressions. See C. Wright Mills, *The Power Elite* (New York: Oxford University Press, 1959); George Grant, *Technology and Empire. Perspectives on North America* (Toronto: House of Anansi, 1969); or Robert Nisbet, *Twilight of Authority* (New York: Oxford University Press, 1975.)

Conclusion

This is the place to summarize, to explain, perhaps to mend a few fences.

What I have tried to design is a historical typology of the Canadian media. My apologies to the historians for some of the liberties the task has forced me to take with the past. I admit the survey sometimes rides roughshod through the thicket of events that makes up history. In particular, I recognize the dangers in generalizing about print journalism, wherein the eccentric ways of publisher or editor ensure an exception to every rule. But simplification, even gross simplification, is necessary to highlight the significance of the media to the shaping of the Canadian experience. The very attention that politicians, business and labour leaders, or churchmen have payed to the media suggests their recognition of the power of communications. Much more so, I might add, than the work of scholars in most of academe. All too often, the historians, whether doing political or economic studies, even social and cultural monographs, have been indifferent to the role the media have played. Newspapers, for example, are well regarded as a source of information about partisan opinion or public affairs, rarely as actors in their own right. The neglect of this dimension of causation results in an unbalanced appraisal of the way things were.

Communications are not, however, the key force in the past or present. Nothing is. Here, I part company with Harold Innis and Marshall McLuhan who have asserted the primacy of communications technology in the making of civilization. My research has uncovered little evidence that "the medium is the message." True, the condition of, say, print technology had some effect on the communications of the press, and the response they evoked from readers. Also, radio by its very nature spanned the distances and so altered people's relationship to their environment. But far more important is the content of the messages and the phenomenon of mass communication. For the images of life that the media disseminated and the size of the audience these images reached are both central to any explanation of the social roles of the media. Moreover, the multimedia may now be the masters of consciousness, but no media have ever been the masters of fate. Always, their power has been mediated. Always, their messages have been conditioned by character and circumstance. The Canadian experience, the particular social reality, is the result of a complex of factors. Why rural Canada was swallowed up in the urban maw has more to do, I suspect, with the factory, the railway, and the internal combustion engine than the newspaper or radio. I am dubious that much more than influence (however defined) can be claimed for the media and communications.

I have here and there in this tale attributed a great deal of influence to the media. The import of the media lies in their production of ideas, stereotypes, and myths that are consumed and shared by the citizenry. This bold explanation, of course, masks a much more complex, and subtle, relationship between the communicators and their culture. The media do not operate in a vacuum. Newspapers, radio, and television, especially when subject to the discipline of the marketplace, must reflect moods and attitudes evident in the country. Again, these media are subject to pressure from the assorted establishments of the day, so likely to uphold, if only in part, the overall values and strategies of the nation's leaders. The importance of the host culture, for example, accounts for the often substantial differences in the character and messages of the anglophone and francophone media. Whatever social reality the media have reflected, though, they have also moulded — whether this term be refined to mean reinforce, legitimate, glorify, enshrine, or alter. Over time, the media do exercise a definite power upon the ways, the rituals, the assumptions, the concerns of the public, which together with much else constitute the social reality. Does this fact make the media a flawed mirror of life? Perhaps so. Better yet, the media are a filter through which certain images of life are purified and enhanced. Media influence, then, is determined by the very ideological and institutional environment the media inform.

The autonomy and influence of the media have grown slowly over the years. The colonial press, for all its vigour, remained the servant of the politicians, businessmen, and churchmen in a still custom-bound British America. Indeed, the cultural schizophrenia of French Québec, a community divided into a literate top and an illiterate bottom, spawned a press that catered almost exclusively to the assorted professional elites struggling for dominance. Even so, the anglophone and francophone press did work to legitimate the making of a Victorian Canada. The situation altered somewhat once industrialism brought in its wake the mass daily. The contact the big city publisher established with a large public gave him prestige, wealth, and at least the illusion of independence. The messages of this publisher broadened the horizons of the public, undermining the isolation of the island communities throughout the land, and fostered interest and class consciousness which supplemented the ethnic and sectional cleavages that also persisted. Of course, the political party and big business, the latter the best organized interest in early twentieth century Canada, enjoyed much say in the news and views of the mass press. Besides, again in Québec, if a vulgar La Presse could claim a huge readership, there flourished as well such Victorian types as Bourassa's elite Le Devoir, the church's L'Action Catholique, and the Liberal Le Canada. And, everywhere in Canada, there were moral media that continued to buttress the traditions of the Victorian order. Only with the triumph of the multimedia have newspapers, radio, and television come to enjoy an independence and a reach that gives their communications a frightening significance. The recent dissolution of the British legacy in English Canada and the Duplessis regime in French Québec was signal evidence of the death of Victorian traditions, just as the collapse of partisanship and the waning prestige of business suggests the declining authority of the old establishment. Not the new, I should emphasize, for the state and its bureaucracy are clearly growing in prominence and power. Still, nowadays, the media are, in the jargon of John Porter and Wallace Clement, the prime locus of power in "the ideological system."

The roles the media have played, nonetheless, display a surprising continuity. First of all, communications in Canada have remained a cosmopolitan influence. The native voices, no matter how lusty, have been an ally and an alternative, on occasion the hapless competitor, of foreign media and messages — from Rome, France, Britain, and especially the United States. What changed was the growing volume of foreign communications, a consequence really of the rise of the multimedia. Thus, foreign ideas have played an extraordinarily prominent part in the formation of Canadian opinion. The country was and is, in many ways, an intellectual colony, undeniably benefiting from the innovations others pioneered. Partly as a result, the Canadian media have been ambiguous agents of nation-building. Admittedly, the media have sponsored the national idea, especially in their views upon public questions. As often, they have worked to emphasize the limited identities — once of city and creed and race, more recently of province and nationality. That has contributed to the anemic sense of national solidarity and the vigour of lesser loyalties which, together with the North American ethos, now underly the Canadian mosaic. Finally, the media have preached the virtues of what, for the sake of brevity, can be called liberal capitalism. That, of course, took many forms, from the Victorian ethos of the colonial press, to the bourgeois democracy of the mass press, and eventually the affluent society of the multimedia. Each of the media systems, though, spread the word to a wider public, engaged more and more people in the mainstream of Canadian life.

This, in particular, points to the impact of the media and their messages upon Canada's open society. I mean thereby a land wherein reason, ideas, and debate amongst the general citizenry play an essential part in the public arena and private life. The importance of the media here lies not just in their dissemination of facts and opinions, or even their discussion of principles. The media have been the abode of orthodoxy, whose influence has often been damned conservative since it reinforces the prevailing patterns of values and authority. No less important, the media have worked to add novelty to the body of conventional wisdom, and so won praise (or notoriety) as a liberal influence that alters these patterns. In fact, both functions serve to maintain the open society: the first ensuring continuity and preserving stability, whilst the second makes for flexibility if not change. It was the colonial newspaper which, in effect, called into being public opinion, albeit limited to the literate, bourgeois citizenry. The mass press fulfilled a double mission by widening the public to include the urban masses, native-born and immigrant, and by transmitting to them the leading values of the age. The multimedia have catered to the organized interests of a plural public and buttressed, especially through advertising and entertainment, a social consensus. The range of opinions expressed, of course, has varied greatly over the years. The 1840s, the 1900s, and the 1960s were characterized by outspoken, even chaotic controversy, in which some form of radicalism was prominent in media comment. Superficially at least, the 1870s, the 1920s, and the 1950s were decades when conformity and agreement seemed to rule in the realm of ideas amongst much of the media. In any case, the maintenance and present vigour of the open society owes much to the contribution of the Canadian media.

That accounts for my lack of sympathy with the critics of the media. Press, radio, television, the cinema, all are imperfect. The charges of excessive business influence, yellow journalism, repetitive entertainment, impoverished news, and gross profits have some justification. There is much about the press or television I too would like to see improved, simply to suit my peculiar tastes. That is the trouble with the reform hysteria. So much of the criticism of the multimedia reflects the special crotchets of the scold. He yearns for his own brand of perfection. If the observations made in this survey appear too sanguine, that is because the media nowadays do supply a worthwhile service to the consumer. What use the consumer makes of the service is up to him. Not that I urge the consumer to adopt a more sophisticated approach to the media. Perhaps a good idea, but hardly necessary. Enjoy the present: it can't, as a favoured cliché warns, last forever.

A Media Bibliography

Abbreviations:

CD: *Les Cahiers des Dix*
CHAR: *Canadian Historical Association Report*
CHR: *Canadian Historical Review*
MM: *Maclean's Magazine or Maclean's*
RS: *Recherches Sociographiques*
TRSC: *Transactions of the Royal Society of Canada*
M&S: McClelland and Stewart
UTP: University of Toronto Press

I General

BEAULIEU, A. and J. Hamelin, *Les Journaux du Québec de 1764 à 1964*, Québec: Les Cahiers de l'Institut d'Histoire, no. 6, 1965 (newspaper locations and descriptions plus a bibliography of sources)

BOORSTIN, D. J. *The Americans. The Democratic Experience*. New York: Random House, 1973.

CAREY, J. W. "Canadian Communication Theory: Extentions and Interpretations of Harold Innis," in G. J. Robinson and D. F. Theall, *Studies in Canadian Communications*. Montreal: McGill University, 1975, pp. 27-59.

DeFLEUR, M. and S. Ball-Rockeach. *Theories of Mass Communication*, 3rd edition. New York: David McKay, 1975.

DUDEK, L. *Literature and the Press: A History of Printing, Printed Media, and Their Relation to Literature*. Toronto: Ryerson, 1960.

ELLIOT, R. "The Canadian Labour Press from 1869: A Chronological Annotated Directory," *Canadian Journal of Economics and Political Science*, 14, 1948, pp. 220-245.

HAMELIN, J. and A. Beaulieu. "Aperçu du journalisme québécoise d'expression française," RS, 7, 1966, pp. 305-346.

HARPER, J. R. *Historical Directory of New Brunswick Newspapers and Periodicals*. Fredericton: University of New Brunswick, 1961.

HOGGART, R. *The Uses of Literacy*. London: Penguin, 1973.

INNIS, H. *The Bias of Communication*. Toronto: UTP, 1951.

INNIS, H. *Empire and Communications*. Toronto: UTP, 1972.

JOHANSEN, P. "Studies in Journalism: An Introductory Bibliography," in G. S. Adam, editor, *Journalism, Communication and the Law*, Scarborough: Prentice-Hall, 1976, pp. 225-241.

KESTERTON, W. *A History of Journalism in Canada*. Carleton Library no. 36. Toronto: M&S, 1967.

KLAPPER, J. *The Effects of Mass Communication*. New York: Free Press, 1960.

LIEBLING, A. J. *The Press*. Second revised edition. New York: Ballantine, 1975.

LUNN, J. "Bibliography of the History of the Canadian Press," CHR, 22, 1941, pp. 416-433.

McLUHAN, M. *Understanding Media. The Extensions of Man*. Scarborough: New American Library, 1964.

McQUAIL, D. *Towards a Sociology of Mass Communications*. London: Collier-Macmillan, 1969.

MILL, J. S. "On Liberty," *Utilitarianism, Liberty and Representative Government*. Everyman's Library no. 452. London: John Dent and Sons Ltd., 1910, . 65-170.

MOTT, F. *American Journalism*. New York: Macmillan, 1962.

POPPER, K. *The Open Society and Its Enemies*. 2 vols, Harper Torchbooks. New York: Harper and Row, 1963.

SIEBERT, F. S., T. Peterson, and W. Schramm. *Four Theories of the Press*. Urbana: University of Illinois Press, 1973.

WILLIAMS, F. *Dangerous Estate. The Anatomy of Newspapers*. London: Arrow Books, 1959 (the British press).

II The Rise of the Newspaper (1750-1870)

AUDET, F.-J. "Adam Thom (1802-1890)." TRSC, series 3, 35, 1941, section 1, pp. 1-12.

BAILLIE, jr., J. "Charles Fothergill 1782-1840." CHR, 25, 1944, pp. 376-396.

BEAULIEU, A. and J. Hamelin, La Presse Québécoise des origines à nos nours, 1: 1764-1859 & 2: 1860-1879. Québec:Les Presses de L'Université Laval, 1973 and 1975.

BLYTH, J. "The Development of the Paper Industry in Old Ontario, 1824-1867." Ontario History, 62, 1970, pp. 119-133.

BRUNET, M. "Les Idées Politiques de la Gazette littéraire de Montreal (1778-1779)," CHAR, 1951, pp. 43-50.

CARELESS, J. M. S. Brown of the Globe. 2 vols. Toronto: Macmillan, 1959 & 1963.

CARELESS, J. M. S. "Mid-Victorian Liberalism in Central Canadian Newspapers, 1850-1867," CHR, 31, pp. 221-236.

COOPER, J. I. "The Early Editorial Policy of the Montreal Witness," CHAR, 1947, pp. 53-62.

ELLIOT, H. editor. Fate, Hope and Editorials. Ottawa: Canadian Library Association, 1967 (synopses of assorted newspapers and their responses to the Confederation issue).

FALARDEAU, J.-C. "Étienne Parent," in Dictionary of Canadian Biography, 10: 1871 to 1880. Toronto: UTP, 1972, pp. 579-587.

FAUCHER, A. "Le Canadien upon the Defensive, 1806-10," CHR, 28, 1947, pp. 249-265.

FAUTEUX, A. "Les débuts de l'imprimerie au Canada," CD, 16, 1951, pp. 17-37.

FIRTH, E. Early Toronto Newspapers, 1793-1867. Toronto: Baxter Publishing, 1955.

GATES, L. F. "The Decided Policy of William Lyon Mackenzie," CHR, 40, 1959, pp. 185-208.

GERVAIS, G. "Un Souverainiste du XIXe siècle: Médéric Lanctôt 1838-1877," RS, 10, 1969, pp. 409-418.

GUNDY, H. P. Early Printers and Printing in Canada. Toronto: Bibliographical Society of Canada, 1957.

GUNDY, H. P. "Liberty and Licence of the Press in Upper Canada." in W. H. Heick and R. Graham, editors, His Own Man. Essays in Honour of Arthur Reginald Marsden Lower. Montreal: McGill-Queen's University Press, 1974, pp. 71-92.

GUNDY, H. P. "Literary Publishing," in K. F. Klinck, editor, Literary History of Canada. Canadian Literature in English. Toronto: UTP, 1966. pp. 174-188.

HAMILTON, W. B. "P. S. Hamilton — The Forgotten Confederate," Collections of the Nova Scotia Historical Society, 36, 1968, pp. 66-94.

HARE, J. and J.-P. Wallot. Les Imprimés dans le Bas-Canada 1801-1810. Montréal: Les Presses de l'Université de Montréal, 1967.

HARPER, J. R. "Christopher Sower King's Printer and Loyalist," New Brunswick Historical Society, Collections, 14, 1955, pp. 67-108.

HAWORTH, E. Imprint of a Nation. Toronto: Baxter Publishing, 1969 (a history of printing in Canada).

HILL, R. A. "A Note on Newspaper Patronage in Canada during the late 1850s and early 1860s," CHR, 49, 1968, pp. 44-59.

KILBOURN, W. The Firebrand. William Lyon Mackenzie and the Rebellion in Upper Canada. Toronto: Clarke Irwin, 1956.

LEFEBVRE, A. Le Montreal Gazette et le nationalisme canadien, 1835-1842. Montréal: Guérin, 1971.

LEMIEUX, D. "Les Mélanges religieux, 1841-52," RS, 10, 1969, pp. 207-236.

LEWIS, M. H. "A Reappraisal of George Sheppard's Contribution to the Press of North America," Ontario History, 62, 1970, pp. 179-198.

MACPHERSON, I. "The Liberal of St. Thomas, Ontario 1832-1833," Western Ontario Historical Notes, 21, 1965, pp. 10-29.

MARTELL, J. S. "Early Parliamentary Reporting in Nova Scotia 1817-1837," CHR, 21, 1940, pp. 284-303.

MARTELL, J. S. "The Press of the Maritime Provinces in the 1830s," CHR, 19, 1938, pp. 24-29.

McLEAN, M. "Early Parliamentary Reporting in Upper Canada," CHR, 20, 1939, pp. 378-391.

MILLER, H. O. "The History of the Newspaper Press in London, 1830-1875," Ontario Historical Society, Papers and Records, 32, 1937, pp. 114-139.

MONTMINY, J.-P. "L'Avenir, 1847-1852," RS, 10, 1969, pp. 323-353.

PIETTE-SAMSON, C. "La représentation ultramontaine de la société à travers Le Courrier du Canada," RS, 10, 1969, pp. 431-437.

PIETTE-SAMSON, C. "Louis-Antoine Dessaulles, journaliste libéral," RS, 10, 1969, pp. 373-387.

ROY, J. A. Joseph Howe: A Study in Achievement and Frustration. Toronto: Macmillan, 1935.

SMITH, A. "Old Ontario and the Emergence of a National Frame of Mind," in F. H. Armstrong, H. A. Stevenson, J. D. Wilson, editors, Aspects of Nineteenth-Century Ontario. Essays Presented to James J. Talman. Toronto: UTP, 1974, pp. 194-217.

SMITH, L. "Le Canadien and the British Constitution, 1806-1810," CHR, 38, 1957, pp. 93-108.

SYLVAIN, P. "Cyrille Boucher (1834-1865) disciple de Louis Veuillot," CD, 37, 1972, pp. 295-317.

SYLVAIN, P. "Les Débuts du 'Courrier du Canada' et les progrès de l'ultramontanisme canadien-français," CD, 32, 1967, pp. 255-278.

TALMAN, J. "George Sheppard, Journalist, 1819-1912," TRSC, series 3, 44, 1950, section 2, pp. 119-134.

TALMAN, J. "The Newspapers of Upper Canada a Century Ago," CHR, 19, 1938, pp. 9-23.

TALMAN, J. "The Newspaper Press of Canada West, 1850-60," TRSC, series 3, 33, 1939, section 2, pp. 149-174.

THOMPSON, S. Reminiscences of a Canadian Pioneer for the Last Fifty Years. Toronto: M&S, 1968.

>TREMAINE, M. A Bibliography of Canadian Imprints 1751-1800. Toronto: UTP, 1952. (contains an excellent introduction on early printing).

TREMBLAY, J.-P. "Un journaliste satirique du Canada français au XIXe siècle: Napoléon Aubin," Revue de l'Université Laval, 20, 1966, pp. 816-831.

VACHON, G.-A. "Une Pensée incarnée," Etudes Françaises, numéro spécial, 5, 1969, pp. 249-258. (early francophone journalism).

WALLACE, W. S. "The Periodical Literature of Upper Canada," CHR, 12, 1931, pp. 4-22 and 181-183.

>WAITE, P. B. The Life and Times of Confederation 1864-1867. Politics, Newspapers, and the Union of British North America. Second edition. Toronto: UTP, 1962.

WISE, S. F. "Sermon Literature and Canadian Intellectual History," United Church of Canada, The Bulletin, 1965, pp. 3-18.

III The Golden Age of the Press (1870-1930)

ANGUS, H. F., editor, Canada and Her Great Neighbor. Sociological Surveys of Opinions and Attitudes in Canada Concerning the United States. Toronto: Ryerson, 1938.

BOUCHARD, G. "Apogée et déclin de l'ideoligie ultramontaine à travers le journal Le Nouveau Monde 1867-1900," RS, 10, 261-291.

BOWMAN, C. A. Ottawa Editor. The Memoirs of Charles A. Bowman. Sidney: Gray's Publishing, 1966.

BRENNAN, J. W. "Press and Party in Saskatchewan, 1914-1929," Saskatchewan History, 27, 1974, pp. 81-94.

BROWN, R. C. "Canadian Nationalism in Western Newspapers," in D. Swainson, editor, Historical Essays on the Prairie Provinces. Carleton Library no. 53. Toronto: M&S, 1970, pp. 90-98.

BRUCE, C. News and the Southams. Toronto: Macmillan, 1968.

CAMPBELL, B. "From Hand-Set Type to Linotype: Reminiscences of Fifty Years in the Printing Trade," British Columbia Historical Quarterly, 10, 1946, 353-372.

CHALMERS, F. S. A Gentleman of the Press. Toronto: Doubleday, 1969 (a biography of J. B. Maclean)

CHARLESWORTH, H. Candid Chronicles: Leaves from the Note Book of a Canadian Journalist. Toronto: Macmillan, 1925.

COLQUHOUN, A. H. U. "The Canadian Press Association," in A History of Journalism in the Several Portions of the Dominion with a Sketch of the Canadian Press Association, 1859-1908, edited by a Committee of the Association, Toronto, 1908, pp. 1-132.

COLQUHOUN, A. H. U. *Press, Politics and People: The Life and Letters of Sir John Willison, Journalist and Correspondent of the Times*, Toronto: Macmillan, 1935.

COOK, R. *The Politics of John W. Dafoe and the Free Press*. Toronto: UTP, 1963.

CRAICK, W. A. *A History of Canadian Journalism*, v. 2, Toronto: Ontario Publishing, 1959. (on the CPA and CDNPA).

CRANSTON, J. H. *Ink on My Fingers*. Toronto: Ryerson, 1953.

DAFOE, J. W. "Early Winnipeg Newspapers," Historical and Scientific Society of Manitoba, *Papers*, 3, 1947, pp. 14-24.

DEMPSEY, H. editor, *The Best of Bob Edwards*. Edmonton: Hurtig, 1975.

DONNELLY, M. *Dafoe of the Free Press*. Toronto: Macmillan, 1968.

DRAKE, E. "Pioneer Journalism in Saskatechewan, 1878-1887," *Saskatchedwan History*, 5, 1952, pp. 17-27 and 41-54.

DUMONT, F., J. Hamelin, F. Harvey, J.-P. Montminy, editors, *Idéologies au Canada français 1900-1929*. Québec: Les Presses de l'Université Laval, 1974 (a variety of newspaper analyses).

EGGLESTON, W. *While I Still Remember. A Personal Record*. Toronto: Ryerson, 1968 (excellent on the Toronto *Star* in the interwar years).

FERGUSON, G. V. *John W. Dafoe*. Toronto: Ryerson, 1948.

GAGNON, M.-A. *La Vie Orageuse d'Olivar Asselin*, 2 vols. Montréal: Editions de l'Homme, 1962.

GODIN, P. *L'Information-Opium. Une Histoire Politique de La Presse*. Montréal: Editions Parti Pris, 1973.

GREENAWAY, R. *The News Game*. Toronto: Clarke Irwin, 1966.

GRIFFIN, F. *Variety Show. Twenty Years of Watching the News Parade*. Toronto: Macmillan, 1936.

HANN, R. "Brainworkers and the Knights of Labour: E. E. Sheppard, Phillips Thompson, and the Toronto *News*, 1883-1887," in G. S. Kealey and P. Warrian, editors, *Essays in Canadian Working Class History*, Toronto: M&S, 1976, pp. 35-57.

HARKNESS, R. J. *E. Atkinson of the Star*. Toronto: UTP, 1963.

JONES, R. *L'Idéologie de L'Action Catholique (1917-1939)*. Québec: Les Presses de l'Université Laval, 1974.

KALBFLEISCH, H. K. *The History of the Pioneer German Language Press of Ontario, 1835-1918*. Toronto: UTP, 1968.

KIRKCONNELL, W. "The European Canadians in Their Press," CHAR, 1940, 85-92.

LAMB, B. "From 'Tickler' to 'Telegram': Notes on Early Vancouver Newspapers," *British Columbia Historical Quarterly*, 9, 1945, pp. 174-199.

LAVOIE, E. "La clientèle du *Courrier du Canada*," *Culture*, 30, 1969, pp. 299-309 and 31, 1970, pp. 40-57.

MILLER, C. "English-Canadian Opposition to the South African War as Seen Through the Press," CHR, 55, 1974, pp. 422-438.

MOFFETT, S. F. *The Americanization of Canada*, Social History of Canada, Toronto: UTP, 1972.

NICHOLS, M. E. *(CP) The Story of the Canadian Press*. Toronto: Ryerson, 1938.

PELLETIER, J.-G. "La Presse Canadienne-Française et la Guerre des Boers," RS, 4, 1963, pp. 337-349.

PERKINS, H. J. "The Origins of the Popular Press," *History Today*, 1957, pp. 425-435 (the British scene).

PETERSON, T. *Magazines in the Twentieth Century*, second edition. Urbana: University of Illinois Press, 1964 (the American scene).

PORTER, M. "The Pulse of French Canada," MM, 15 March 1954, pp. 18-19, 63-64, 67-68 (on *La Presse*).

POULTON, R. *The Paper Tyrant. John Ross Robertson of the Toronto Telegram*. Toronto: Clarke Irwin, 1971.

ROSS, P.D. *Retrospects of a Newspaper Person*. Toronto: Oxford, 1931.

RUTHERFORD, P. "The People's Press: The Emergence of the New Journalism in Canada, 1869-1899," CHR, 56, 1975, pp. 167-191.

RUTHERFORD, P. "The Western Press and Regionalism, 1870-96," CHR, 52, 1971, pp. 287-305.

SAVARD, P. *Jules-Paul Tardivel, La France et les Etats-Unis, 1851-1905*. Québec: Les Presses du l'Université Laval, 1967.

SAVARD, P. "Jules-Paul Tardivel, un ultramontain devant les problemes et les hommes de son temps," CHAR, 1963, pp. 125-140.

SECCOMBE, W. W. A Private Concern. Willowdale: Nelson, Foster and Scott, 1974.

SILVER, A. I. "Some Quebec Attitudes in an Age of Imperialism and Ideological Conflict," CHR, 57, 1976, pp. 440-460.

SMITH, I. N. The Journal Men. Three Great Canadian Newspapermen and the Tradition They Created. Toronto: M&S, 1974.

ST. ARNAUD, P. "La Patrie, 1879-1880," RS, 10, 1969, pp. 355-373.

STEELE, C. F. Prairie Editor. The Life and Times of Buchanan of Lethbridge. Toronto: Ryerson, 1940.

THERIO, A. Jules Fournier, journaliste de combat. Montréal: Fides, 1954.

TREMBLAY, L. Entre Deux Livraisons, 1913-1963. Ottawa: Le Droit, 1963 (on Le Droit of Ottawa).

TROFIMENKOFF, S. M. Action Française: French-Canadian Nationalism in the Twenties. Toronto: UTP, 1975.

TUREK, V. The Polish Language Press in Canada. Its History and a Bibliographical List. Toronto: Polish Alliance Press, 1962.

WADDELL, W. S. "Frank Oliver and the Bulletin," Alberta Historical Review, 5, 1957, pp. 7-12.

WARD, N. "The Press and the Patronage: An Exploratory Operation," in J. H. Aitchison, editor, The Political Process in Canada: Essays in Honour of R. MacGregor Dawson. Toronto: UTP, 1966, pp. 3-16.

WATT, F. W. "Literature of Protest," in H. F. Klinck, editor, Literary History of Canada. Canadian Literature in English. Toronto: UTP, 1966, pp. 457-473.

WILLISON, J. S. Reminiscences Personal and Political. Toronto: M&S, 1919.

WOLFE, M., editor. A Saturday Night Scrapbook. Toronto: New Press, 1973.

IV The Triumph of the Multimedia (1920-1975)

ADAM, G. S. "The Sovereignty of the Publicity System: A Case Study of the Alberta Press Act," in G. S. Adam, editor, Journalism, Communication and the Law. Scarborough: Prentice-Hall, 1976, pp. 154-171.

BARNOUW, E. A History of Broadcasting in the United States, 3 vols. Oxford, 1966, 1968, 1970.

BARRIS, A. The Pierce-Arrow Showroom is Leaking. An Insider's View of the CBC. Toronto: Ryerson, 1969 (on CBC light entertainment).

BLACK, C. "The Fourth Estate," Duplessis. Toronto: M&S, 1977, pp. 639-659.

BLACK, E. R. "Canadian Public Policy and the Mass Media," Canadian Journal of Economics, 1, 1968, pp. 368-379.

BRIGGS, A. A History of Broadcasting in the United Kingdom, 3 vols. Oxford, 1961, 1965, 1970.

BERTON, P. "The Amazing Career of George McCullagh." MM, 15 January, 1949, pp. 8-9 & 42-44.

BERTON, P. "Hindmarsh of the Star." MM, 1 April 1952, pp. 16-17, 37-40, & 42.

BERTON, P. Hollywood's Canada. The Americanization of Our National Image. Toronto: M&S, 1975.

BERTON, P. "Vancouver's Rising Sun," MM, 1 July 1947, pp. 7 & 39-41.

BRADDON, R. Roy Thomson of Fleet Street. London: Collins, 1965.

CALLWOOD, J. "The Truth about Parliament," MM, 17 April 1965, pp. 9-11, 42-46, & 49-50 (on the Press Gallery).

CAMERON, A. D. and J. A. Hannigan "Mass Communications in a Canadian City," in B. D. Singer, editor, Communications in Canadian Society, second revised edition, Toronto: Copp Clark, 1975, pp. 71-90.

CANADA, Committee on Broadcasting. Report, 1965. Ottawa: Queen's Printer, 1965.

CANADA, Royal Commision on National Development in the Arts, Letters and Sciences 1949-1951. Report. Ottawa: King's Printer, 1951.

CANADA, Royal Commission on Publications. Report. Ottawa: Queen's Printer, 1961.

CANADA, Special Senate Committee on Mass Media, Report, 3 vols. Ottawa: Queen's Printer, 1970.

CAPLAN, G. "The Battle," The Dilemma of Canadian Socialism. The CCF in Ontario. Toronto: M&S, 1973, pp110-133 (an account of anti-CCF propaganda).

CHARLESWORTH, H. *I'm Telling You. Being the Further Candid Chronicles.* Toronto: Macmillan, 1937 (on his radio experiences).

CLAYRE, A. *The Impact of Broadcasting or, Mrs. Buckle's Wall is Singing.* London: Compton Russell, 1973 (the British scene).

CLEMENT, W. "The Media Elite: Gatekeepers of Ideas" and "Structure and Concentration of Canada's Mass Media," *The Canadian Corporate Elite. An Analysis of Economic Power,* Carleton Library no. 89. Toronto: M&S, 1975, pp. 270-343.

COTE, J. *La Communication au Québec.* Repentigny: Les Editions Point de Mire, 1974.

CREAN, S. M. *Who's Afraid of Canadian Culture?* Don Mills: General Publishing, 1976.

CUMMING, C. "The Canadian Press: A Force for Consensus," in G. S. Adam, editor, *Journalism, Communication and the Law.* Scarborough: Prentice-Hall, 1976, pp. 86-103.

DAGNEAU, G.-H. "Remarques sur l'influence des quotidiens de langue française au Canada," *Culture,* 8, 1947, pp. 243-253.

DEMPSON, P. *Assignment Ottawa. Seventeen Years in the Press Gallery.* Toronto: General Publishing, 1968.

DONNEUR, A.-P. "La presse du Québec et les pays étrangers," *Etudes Internationales,* 3, 1971, pp. 410-423.

EGGLESTON, W. "The Press of Canada," in Canada, Royal Commission on National Development in the Arts, Letters and Sciences, 1949-1951, *Royal Commission Studies.* Ottawa: King's Printer, 1951, pp. 41-53.

ELKIN, F. *Rebels and Colleagues. Advertising and Social Change in French Canada.* Montreal: McGill-Queen's University Press, 1973.

FARIS, R. *The Passionate Educators. Voluntary Associations and the Struggle for Control of Adult Educational Broadcasting in Canada 1919-52.* Toronto: Peter Martin Associates, 1975.

FINANCIAL POST. "Report on Media," 1 May, 1976.

FIRESTONE, O. J. *Broadcast Advertising in Canada. Past and Future Growth.* Ottawa: University of Ottawa Press, 1966.

FRASER, B. "The vast and turbulent empire of the Siftons." MM, 5 December 1959, pp. 15-17 and 83-86.

FRASER, B. "Our Hush, Hush Censorship. How Books are Banned." MM, 15 December 1949, pp. 24-25 & 44.

FREMONT, D. "La presse de langue française au Canada," in Canada, Royal Commission on National Development in the Arts, Letters and Sciences, 1949-51, *Royal Commission Studies.* Ottawa: King's Printer, 1951, pp. 55-66.

FULFORD, R. *Marshall Delaney at the Movies. The Contemporary World as Seen on Films.* Toronto: Peter Martin Associates, 1974.

FULFORD, R. "The Press in the Community," in D. B. L. Hamlin, editor, *The Press and the Public.* Toronto: UTP, 1962, pp. 23-34.

GARNER, H. "Remember when we raved about radio?" MM, 1 September 1956, pp. 18-21 & 46-50.

GAUL, W. "Censors in Celluloid." MM, 15 June 1940, pp. 10 & 38-40.

HALLMAN, E. S. with H. Hindley. *Broadcasting in Canada.* Don Mills: General Publishing, 1977.

HENDRY, P. *Epitaph for Nostalgia. A Personal Memoir on the Death of the Family Herald.* Montreal: Agri-World Press, 1968.

HUNT, R. and R. Campbell. *K. C. Irving The Art of the Industrialist.* Toronto: M&S, 1973.

HUTCHISON, B. *The Far Side of the Street.* Toronto: Macmillan, 1976.

HUTTON, E. "How John Bassett, Corporate Executive, Became a Celebrity." MM, 19 May 1962, pp. 20 & 69-71.

IRVING, J., editor. *Mass Media in Canada.* Toronto: Ryerson, 1962.

JAMIESON, D. *The Troubled Air.* Fredericton: Brunswick Press, 1966 (broadcasting in Canada).

JARVIE, J. C. *Towards a Sociology of the Cinema.* London: Routledge and Kegan Paul, 1970.

JOHANNSON, P. R. "Canada's Rock Music Industry: Counterweight or Component of Continentalism?" Association for Canadian Studies in the United States, *Newsletter,* 2, 1972, pp. 35-57.

JOHNSTON, J. G. *The Weeklies: Biggest Circulation in Town.* Bolton: Leavens Printers and Publishers, 1972.

JOHNSTONE, K. "Who'll Le Devoir Battle Next?" MM, 14 April 1956, pp. 36-37 & 94-99.

JOWETT, G. Film. The Democratic Art. Boston: Little Brown, 1976 (superb study of Hollywood in the American context).

JOWETT, G. and B. R. Hemmings. "The Growth of the Mass Media in Canada," in B. D. Singer, editor, Communications in Canadian Society, second revised edition. Toronto: Copp Clark, 1975, pp. 244-266.

KATZ, S. "How Toronto's Evening Papers Slanted the Election News." MM, 15 August 1949, pp. 10-11 & 53-54.

KESTERTON, W. The Law and the Press in Canada, Carleton Library no. 100. Toronto: M&S, 1976.

KIRSCHBAUM, J. M. et al. Twenty Years of the Ethnic Press Association of Ontario. Toronto: The Ethnic Press Association of Ontario, 1971.

KIRSH, C. et al. A Leisure Study – Canada 1972. Toronto: Culturcan, 1973.

KNIGHT, A. The Liveliest Art. A Panoramic History of the Movies. Mentor Books, 1957.

KNOTT, L. "Publishing Problem Child," Canadian Business, August 1949, pp. 21-23 & 80-83 (New Liberty and Jack Kent Cooke).

LANTOS, R. "Fabrication Factories," in D. Macdonald, editor, the media game. Montreal: Content Publishing, 1972, pp. 39-48 (the weekly tabloid press).

LAVOIE, E. "L'Evolution de la Radio au Canada Français avant 1940," RS, 12, 1971, pp. 17-49.

LITVAK, I. and C. Maule. Cultural Sovereignty. The Time and Reader's Digest Case in Canada. New York: Praeger Publishers, 1974.

MAISTRE, G. "Aperçu socio-économique de la presse quotidienne québécoise," RS, 12, 1971, pp. 105-115.

MAISTRE, G. "L'influence de la radio et de la télévision Américanes au Canada," RS, 12, 1971, pp. 51-75.

McDAYTER, W. and R. Elman. "In the Shadow of Giants: Concentration and Monopolies in the Media," in W. McDayter, editor, A Media Mosaic: Canadian Communications Through a Critical Eye. Toronto: Holt, Rinehart and Winston, 1971.

McLUHAN, M. The Mechanical Bride. Folklore of Industrial Man. Boston: Beacon Press, 1967.

McNAUGHT, C. Canada Gets the News. Toronto: Ryerson, 1940 (a superb study of the prewar press).

MILLWARD, A. "The Press," The Canada Year Book. Ottawa: King's Printer, 1939, pp. 737-777.

MOUSSEAU, M. Analyse des Nouvelles Télévisées. Ottawa: Information Canada, 1970.

NIXON, R. B. and J.-H. Huhn. "Concentration of Press Ownership: A Comparison of 32 Countries," Journalism Quarterly, Spring 1971, pp. 5-16.

PACKARD, V. The Hidden Persuaders. New York: Pocket Books, 1957 (the techniques of advertising).

PEERS, F. "Oh say, can you see?," in I. Lumsden, editor, Close the 49th Parallel Etc. The Americanization of Canada. Toronto: UTP, 1970, pp. 135-156 (the Americanization of broadcasting).

PEERS, F. The Politics of Canadian Broadcasting 1920-1951. Toronto: UTP, 1969.

PENTON, M. J. "The Battle of the Air Waves," Jehovah's Witnesses in Canada. Champions of Freedom of Speech and Worship. Toronto: Macmillan, 1976, pp. 94-110.

PORTER, J. "The Ideological System: The Mass Media," The Vertical Mosaic. An Analysis of Social Class and Power in Canada. Toronto: UTP, 1965.

POTTER, D. "The Institution of Abundance: Advertising," People of Plenty. Economic Abundance and the American Character. Chicago: University of Chicago Press, 1954.

PRANG, M. "The Origins of Public Broadcasting in Canada," CHR, 46, 1965, pp. 1-31.

QUALTER, T. H. and K. A. MacKirdy. "The Press of Ontario and the Election," in J. Meisel, editor, Papers on the 1962 Election. Toronto: UTP, pp. 145-168.

ROBERT, M. "Everything that's fit to print in every language fit to read." MM, 18 June 1960, pp. 25 & 54-57 (the ethnic press).

ROBERTS, K. Leisure. London: Longman, 1970 (an excellent study of the nature of modern leisure).

ROSENBERG, B. and D. M. White, editors. Mass Culture. The Popular Arts in America. New York: Free Press, 1957.

SANDWELL, B. K. "Present Day Influences on Canadian Society," in Canada, Royal Commission on National Development in the Arts, Letters and Sciences, 1949-51, *Royal Commission Studies*. Ottawa: King's Printer, 1951, pp. 1-11.

SAYWELL, J., editor, *Canadian Annual Review*, 1960-1970. Toronto: UTP (the articles on journalism, later mass media, mostly by W. H. Kesterton).

SPEARS, B. "Canadian Newspaper Practice," in Canada, Special Senate Committee on Mass Media, *Good, Bad, or Simply Inevitable?*. Ottawa: Queen's Printer, 1970, pp. 187-207.

STEPHENSON, B. "The Wonderful World of French-Canadian TV." MM, 8 June 1957, pp. 18-19 & 82-85.

STEPHENSON, H. E. and C. McNaught. *The Story of Advertising in Canada: A Chronicle of the Years*. Toronto: Ryerson, 1940.

STEWART, S. *A Pictorial History of Radio in Canada*. Toronto: Gage, 1975.

STURSBERG, P. *Mister Broadcasting. The Ernie Bushnell Story*. Toronto: Peter Martin Associates, 1971.

STURSBERG, P. *Those were the Days, the Days of Benny Nicholas and the Lotus Eaters*. Toronto: Peter Martin Associates, 1969 (Depression journalism at the Victoria *Times*).

THOMSON, Lord, of Fleet. *After I Was Sixty*. Scarborough: Thomas Nelson and Sons, 1975.

TOOGOOD, A. F. *1919-1969: Canadian Broadcasting in Transition*. Ottawa: Canadian Association of Broadcasters, 1969 (contains a good bibliography).

WALKER, D. "Magazines in Canada," in Canada, Special Senate Committee on Mass Media, *Good, Bad, or Simply Inevitable?* Ottawa: Queen's Printer, 1970, pp. 209-240.

WARNOCK, J. "All the News It Pays to Print," in I. Lumsden, editor, *Close the 49th Parallel Etc. The Americanization of Canada*. Toronto: UTP, 1970, pp. 117-134 (the Americanization of the press).

WEAVER, R. "Paperback Revolution," *Queen's Quarterly*, Spring 1955, pp. 70-79.

WEAVER, R. "Two-Bit Culture," *Canadian Forum*, July 1953, pp.78-82.

WEINTRAUB, W. *Why Rock the Boat*. Boston: Little Brown, 1961 (a novel about Montreal journalism).

WEIR, E. A. *The Struggle for National Broadcasting in Canada*. Toronto: M&S, 1965.

YOUNG, B. J. "C. George McCullagh and the Leadership League," in *Politics of Discontent*. Toronto: UTP, 1967, pp. 77-102.

ZOLF, L. *Dance of the Dialectic*. Toronto: James Lewis & Samuel, 1973 (irreverent treatment of the Press Gallery).

Index